From fear to respect
Young people's views on violence

Sue Sharpe

national
children's
bureau
making a difference

NCB's mission and aims

NCB promotes the voices, interests and well-being of all children and young people across every aspect of their lives.

NCB aims to:
- challenge disadvantage in childhood
- work with children and young people to ensure they are involved in all matters that affect their lives
- promote multidisciplinary cross-agency partnerships and good practice
- influence government through policy development and advocacy
- undertake high quality research and work from an evidence-based perspective
- disseminate information to all those working with children and young people, and to children and young people themselves

Published by the National Children's Bureau, Registered Charity number 258825. 8 Wakley Street, London EC1V 7QE. Tel: 020 7843 6000. Website: www.ncb.org.uk

© National Children's Bureau, 2004

ISBN 1 904787 06 1

British Library Cataloguing in Publication Data
A catalogue record for this book is available from the British Library

Contents

Foreword

As this 'thinkpiece' demonstrates, violence and safety are significant and complex issues which impact on the everyday lives of children and young people. Young people must feel safe to learn, safe to play, safe to be themselves, safe to make a mistake, safe to ask for help and advice and safe to be different. They must also be aware of the real and perceived dangers that they are exposed to and be supported to manage the risks and dangers effectively. They need help in being safe and feeling safe.

Personal, Social and Health Education and Citizenship in schools provide a positive and important curriculum opportunity for exploring violence, risk and personal safety. We must listen to, respond to and work with young people if we are truly to achieve our goal of offering safe and positive environments in which all children and young people can flourish. Now, as then, the recommendations and priority areas set out by the Calouste Gulbenkian Foundation in 1995 remain a priority if children and young people are to have a positive start in life.

Simon Blake
National Children's Bureau
May 2004

Acknowledgements

The research that this 'thinkpiece' is based on was a collective endeavour involving the author Sue Sharpe, Janet Holland, Sheila Henderson, Sheena McGrellis and Rachel Thomson. Simon Blake and Rachel Thomson provided editorial support for the publication.

Thanks are due to the Laing Foundation and the Calouste Gulbenkian Foundation for funding the preparation and publication of the report.

Background

Children and young people have the right to feel safe in the home, at school, on the streets and in the community. This is a very important concern, as they themselves express: for example, in the survey by the Office for Children's Rights Commissioner for London, *Sort It Out* (Sharpe 2002a), violence and safety on the streets, and bullying, were high on their list of concerns to be addressed in London.

The following statistics demonstrate the relevance of exploring and addressing violence and safety with young people.

- **Violence in the home (including domestic violence and physical punishment)** – An NCH study in 1994 found 75 per cent of mothers said their children had witnessed domestic violence, 33 per cent of children had seen their mothers beaten up, and 10 per cent had witnessed sexual violence (Women's Aid Federation of England website).
- **Suicide and self-harm** – 10 per cent of teenagers aged 15–16 have deliberately self-harmed, and girls are nearly four times more likely to self-harm than boys. Of those who self-harm, 41 per cent seek help from friends before acting. More than 24,000 teenagers are admitted to hospital in the UK each year after deliberately harming themselves (Samaritans).
- **Guns, air weapons, knives and other weapons** – Firearms, including air weapons, were used in 0.4 per cent of all recorded crime, resulting in 97 fatalities and 558 serious injuries in 2001–02 (Flood-Page and Taylor, 2003). The 2002 Mirror/GMTV/Crimestoppers poll of 1,064 young people found that 2 per cent of the sample had been a victim of a crime involving guns or knives (*The Mirror* 2002).
- **Alcohol and substance misuse** – Young people aged 16–24 are more likely to report 'hazardous' drinking patterns ('hazardous' refers to levels of drinking

and associated behaviour such as impulsivity, risk taking, becoming involved in arguments or having accidents) (Office for National Statistics 2000).

- **Sexual or physical abuse (by adults or young people, either within the home, or by strangers)** – Research suggests that between 25–40 per cent of all sexual assaults are perpetrated by juveniles.
- **Crime and antisocial behaviour** – 61 per cent of offenders in mobile phone thefts are aged under 18, with the peak age being 16. Those aged under 18 constituted 48 per cent of victims of mobile phone thefts, with the peak number of victims being 15–16 years old (20 per cent) (Harrington and Mayhew 2001).
- **Bullying, racism and homophobia** – A study in 2000 showed that in any year 75 per cent of pupils are bullied, but that repeated and severe bullying is likely to be perpetrated and suffered by around 7 per cent of pupils (Glover and others 2000). Of gay men, lesbians and bisexuals surveyed, 82 per cent had been verbally abused and 60 per cent reported being hit or kicked during their time at school (GALOP 1997).
- **Child deaths and abductions** – In 2001/02, there were a total of 76 homicide victims under 16 years of age, a decrease of 24 per cent on the previous year. Of these victims, 57 per cent were killed by their parents, and 12 per cent were the victims of suspects known to them. Only eight of the victims were known to have been killed by strangers and as of October 2002 there were no suspects for 16 of the victims (Flood-Page and Taylor 2003). In 2000, 262 cases of abduction were recorded in England and Wales, and children generally know their abductor (Home Office 2001).
- **Violence and harassment through the Internet, email and text messaging** – An NCH survey in 2002 found that one in four young people are bullied or threatened via their mobile phone or online. Sixteen per cent of young people received bullying or threatening text messages, 7 per cent were harassed in Internet chat rooms, and 4 per cent by email (NCH website).

In 1995 the Calouste Gulbenkian Foundation published a report, *Children and Violence, the report of the Commission on Children and Violence.* This report identified the importance of working towards a non-violent society. The Commission recommended three key priorities:

- making an active commitment to non-violence, including coordinating a UK-wide strategy against violence
- legal reforms, including reforms on punishing children and addressing bullying

- ensuring adequate support and services for children and their families, with a particular focus on inequality and poverty.

Alongside these a number of other issues were identified such as the role of the media in promoting non-violent approaches. While progress has been made in some of these areas, it is recognised that there is a great deal still to be done. In the UK there is an increasing recognition of the importance of listening to the views of children and young people. In working towards a non-violent society and looking at policies and programmes to reduce violence for young people, such as fighting, bullying and community violence, we need to be aware of the meanings of violence in young people's everyday lives and how these relate to those of the adults seeking to do something about it.

1   Introduction

It is said that we live in a society that is getting increasingly violent. This is an awareness reflected down through the generations, as adults tell young people that there was never as much in their own youth. Although to some extent this is looking back to some 'golden age' that may have never existed, the many areas of violence encountered by young people today cannot be denied. Whether as participants or observers, violence is clearly part of many young people's lives, at home, at school, in the street, and as part of the general community in certain areas. This 'thinkpiece' concentrates on the views and experiences of young people themselves. It examines a number of issues related to violence in the family; and through bullying; fighting; community violence and in the media, in order to throw light on the meaning and significance of violence in their lives. It explores what legitimates such violence for them; how young people's moral values about the rights and wrongs of violence clash with their lived experiences; how their attitudes and views may be the same or different from those of adults; and how living in cultures characterised by violence or non-violence create different moral perspectives.

Research on children's and young people's views on violence

The subject of social violence amongst children has been addressed in theory and practice in various disciplines. A study that surveyed over 2,000 schools throughout England showed that pupils are the most vulnerable group of people in school and more likely to face assault and violence from other pupils than outsiders (Gill and Hearnshaw 1997). A more recent MORI poll (2000) showed that 57 per cent of children in school worry about being the victim of physical assault, 55 per cent are afraid of being a victim of theft, and 42 per cent fear bullying. The Calouste Gulbenkian Foundation has a particular interest in this and produced a comprehensive report on children and violence in 1995, with a view to making children's and young people's lives safer.

Although there has been a lot of research over the years on the incidence and possible causes of violence in the family, school and community, there have been relatively few studies that look more specifically at the views of children and young people themselves. There have, however, been some that are relevant to the aspects of violence covered here. These include a survey by Katz, Buchanan and Bream (2001) which documented the views, experiences and backgrounds of young people around bullying, and a DfES funded study recommended anti-bullying strategies (Oliver and Candappa 2003) which used children's views and participation to construct an anti-bullying pack for schools. Willow and Hyder (1999) talked to groups of four- to seven-year-olds to find their views on smacking by parents. Campbell (1989) talked to girls about fighting and girl gangs some years ago, and more recently Michele Burman and others (Burman, Brown and Batchelor 2003) explored the meaning of violence for girls. Research on boys and masculinity (Frosh, Phoenix and Pattman 2002) included violence and homophobia. Other researchers such as Kelly (2002) have sought the views on violence of young people in Northern Ireland on living with sectarianism. When in 2001 the Office for Children's Rights Commissioner for London conducted a survey of London's children, it was found that violence and safety on the streets was the most frequently voiced concern requiring action, closely followed by child abuse, drugs, bullying and racism (Sharpe 2002a). The project on which this 'thinkpiece' is based was a major study which covered a variety of issues and in which the ideas and experiences of the young people participating were central. It was called the Respect study.

The Respect study

Social change is strongly related to the nature of people's values. This exploration of young people's attitudes to aspects of violence is based largely around some of the responses of young people from England and Northern Ireland who took part in a study of moral values in 1996–1999.

The Respect study was a project commissioned by the Economic and Social Research Council in 1996 (entitled *Youth values: identity, diversity and social change*, www.sbu.ac.uk/fhss/ff/). It was a major study involving over 1,700 young people aged 11–16 and used a range of methods to generate rich data about the lives, loves, hopes and fears of young people growing up in the UK today. I was part of the Respect research team and our aim was to understand more about the relationship between what young people value, their identities and their social environments. As part of this we examined how young people understand the processes of their own moral development and how they deal with different contemporary values. We explored the part played by age, gender, ethnicity, religion, social class, type of family and the vital contributions of location, place and community in the construction of young people's moral identity. The Respect study made a point of comparing various locations, and was carried out in schools in five contrasting sites: Northern Ireland; inner-city London; a Home Counties commuter belt town; a rural village in the east of England; and a disadvantaged estate in the North of England. In Northern Ireland, four schools of varying religious predominance took part (one Catholic, one Protestant, and two mixed). In the historical and present-day context of religious conflict in this area, young people living there face a rather different social and political reality from that in England, and it was felt important to explore the impact of this on their values, and their attitudes and expectations around violence. Therefore quite a significant proportion of the material quoted here comes from the Northern Irish young people.

Research methods

One of the main methods that produced the material referred to here was an extensive questionnaire to all participants. The questionnaire provided quantitative and qualitative data which, in the context of 'violence', gave us information on the morality of violence-related activities; the circumstances in which the young people considered that it can be alright to use violence; dilemmas faced by young people in everyday life; levels of agreement/disagreement about violence with parents, friends and teachers. We also asked for a current story or joke going around, and this provided us with a number of jokes that included a violent content. (More detailed information about the questionnaire results of this research can be found in *Through the moral maze* by McGrellis and others (2000) (www.sbu.ac.uk/fhss/ff/).

Focus group discussions were carried out with a selection of the young people who had volunteered to take part in these discussions. The young people were asked about various moral issues around violence, which were explored through some of the contentious statements used to provoke discussion in many of these groups. The focus groups provided a rich source of material (from a total of 56 groups). As well as the groups carried out in schools, several other groups were held, with, for example, a gay and lesbian group, young people in care, and young people in a pupil referral unit. Some of these were slightly older (17–18). In these groups, provocative statements were discussed, including a subset related to violence, parental discipline, bullying, and video computer games. These were: 'Sometimes violence is the only way to get things done'; 'Violence is the only way to get respect'; 'Parents should not have the right to hit their children'; 'Being bullied toughens you up'; and 'Computer games encourage violence'. A number of in-depth individual interviews provided some further attitudes and views.

Aspects of violence from the Respect study

Inasmuch as this project covered diverse kinds of moral values and did not focus particularly on violence, it was significant how much seemed to feature in these young people's lives. This diversity also meant that rather than being comprehensive, not all categories of violence could be explored within the limits of the study. Thus the violence in young people's lives covered in this 'thinkpiece' include: aspects of 'violence' at home, such as parental punishment, conflict between siblings, and between parents; bullying; fighting, such as that triggered through self-defence, personal or family honour, or reputation; community violence, such as that generated by religious differences in Northern Ireland, and local gangs in England; and a chapter on some of the violence represented in the media, such as in computer video games. It was inevitable that some aspects of violence overlap, for example, bullying and fighting are closely related, and fighting and community violence are hard to separate, but the focus in each chapter is more on what is most characteristic of the particular aspect.

In giving their judgements on many ethical issues in the Respect questionnaire data, the majority of the young people were disapproving of physical violence in general. This was particularly the case with issues like fighting with police, using violence for political ends, and carrying a weapon, when half or more of them considered such actions to be always or usually wrong. Bullying was similarly opposed. There was more diversity about issues like taking revenge and fighting, as is clearly reflected in their views and experiences. But it was a different matter when it came to using violence for self-defence, and over two thirds of them (69 per cent) thought this was never or rarely wrong.

It is clear that factors like gender, age and location, are important. For instance, many forms and causes of violence are embedded within particular forms of masculinity. One example lies in a form of masculinity that has its roots, especially for working-class communities, in a traditionally physical expression (Willis 1977, Cohen 1997). It is significant that there are many quotes in this 'thinkpiece' from young men about aspects of violence, whereas on many other issues, such as sex and relationships, it is young women who have more to say. Most violence is committed by males, and this is clear in the representation of bullying, fighting, and community violence described in the later chapters. But girls and young women are also involved, both as instigators and recipients. There are gender contradictions to be found, as traditional views of femininity come up against local situations of aggression. In terms of location, Northern Ireland is clearly a site of extreme political feelings and violence, while the violence characterising certain run-down areas in Northern England is based in a localised gang culture and a context of disadvantage and hardship. Young people from both of these areas participated in the study, and the levels of violence they encountered were significantly higher than in other locations.

This 'thinkpiece' illuminates some of these issues through exploring the views and experiences of the young people in the Respect project, and it is their voices that are heard throughout. Violence was generally seen as morally wrong, but in a world that seems increasingly characterised by violence, it is clear that any simple or blanket disapproval must mask a very complex issue. The relative 'immorality' of violence and advocacy of non-violence is set against the apparent 'necessity' of violence in certain contexts and environments. It is not always possible to ignore or 'say no' to violence, and walk away from it, but there may be ways in which this can be approached which takes account of the meanings and finer nuances that adults may not always pick up on. The conflicts, contradictions and rationalisations in young people's views and behaviours are explored in the following chapters, and it is hoped that this 'thinkpiece' will be useful in informing policies and practice that can change these situations.

To preserve the anonymity of the young people involved in the Respect study we have not used their real names in this report.

2 Violence at home

> They do have the right to hit them but some parents overdo
> it. A wee slap, that's all they should get.
>
> *(Ella, aged 16)*

Domestic violence has been the focus of very many enquiries and research, which
has described the relatively high incidence of violence in the family, between
parents, and between parents and children. Some studies such as McGee (1997,
2000) have explored children's experiences of domestic violence. Although
violence was discussed in a variety of contexts, it was not intended in the Respect
project to ask directly about experiences of physical or sexual abuse, and
correspondingly these were generally not forthcoming. It would in any case have
not been very appropriate for young people to reveal these in a questionnaire or
focus group. Therefore this chapter focuses on some aspects of 'violence' at home,
mainly parental discipline, and the accommodation of violence within the family.

Punishment from adults

> 'Cause you need discipline because like if well, you're not
> told and there is no discipline, well you think you can do
> whatever you want and you'll get into trouble a lot more.
>
> *(Cynthia, aged 13)*

In relation to what constitutes an 'acceptable' level of violence towards children
from parents, views vary from zero tolerance to a certain degree of physical
punishment that includes smacking. Willow and Hyder(1999) carried out a
consultation exercise in 1998 to find out children's views on smacking. They found
that these four- to seven-year-olds defined a smack as involving force and pain and
they described the physical and emotional hurt it caused, and the negative

relationship it caused with parents. Almost all the children said that smacking was wrong, but when asked if they would smack children when they were big, only half of those responding said they would not do this. The authors suggest that they are already picking up signals that this is the approved way to resolve conflicts in the family. In relation to this, the 11- to 17-year-olds taking part in the Respect study seemed to show that these signals had been taken to heart.

In some of the Respect focus groups, the contentious topic under discussion was 'Parents should not have the right to hit their children'. This evoked general agreement that parents should not have this as a right, but their responses were often qualified. There was frequently an in-built contradiction in that although such violence was not seen to be good, and talking would be a better way, there had to be some discipline or else the child would grow up being bad in some way. Roseanne thought that not hitting children when they were bad would mean they would grow up continuing to do these things:

> They have the right to hit their children if the children are bad or something like that, you just can't let them off with anything. But if you're hitting them for no reason, I think that's abuse. They don't have the right to do that, but if they are bad and keep on doing things – if you don't hit your children when they're bad, they're going to get spoilt and keep on doing it.
> *(Roseanne, aged 13)*

They tended to agree that low level physical admonishment was admissible and even necessary for moral development when a child was younger, but as they got older there should be negotiation instead. The acquisition of moral autonomy was closely linked to the development of physical and emotional competence (Thomson and others 2001). They could define boundaries in parenting between violence they consider 'normal', acceptable and necessary, and other kinds that go beyond this (Holland and others 2000). They saw the boundaries of appropriate parenting shifting with age:

> I think like when there's a wain and when it does something wrong it should be smacked on the hand, or the bum, but when they grow up and they're getting hit and all, at 15, 16, I don't think that's right. Should be able to sit down and talk to them, and they should listen, like.
> *(Aideen, aged 14)*

The level of punishment thought to be appropriate therefore often depended on the age of the child, the seriousness of the misdemeanour involved, and the level of punishment (violence) used by the parent. For example, some thought smacking was acceptable for younger children, but not older ones, for whom either a harsher punishment would be more effective, or verbal negotiation. Some could define what they considered as 'suitable' violence/punishment at a certain age or for a certain sort of misdemeanour, for example, Roma thought a hand slap more appropriate for being rude, but a 'hiding' for breaking a window:

> See after about five or something, if they told their Ma to do something, told her to f…. off, or something like that there, the ma just, you know, get the hand and tap them, aye, a wee smack, but see when they get older, say about 14, they should be calmed down but you see some people they just go out and they go totally mad…Well, if you were doing something, say if some man comes – you've smashed a window and you're out to all hours, and then he comes knocking at your door and all, I think you deserve a hiding for that.
> *(Roma, aged 15)*

For Nadia, physical punishment was also more appropriate for more serious wrongdoings like stealing:

> **Interviewer:** In what situation is it OK to hit?
> **Nadia:** Just say they were caught stealing or something.
> **Lydia:** No, silly things like –
> **Nadia:** – like stealing or bullying or something.
> *(12–13-year-olds)*

And Rory thought a 'little bashing' was appropriate punishment for mugging old ladies!

> If he keeps getting himself like nicked – he's going out mugging old ladies then that's different you know what I mean? You've got to give him a little bashing. But if he's just like being rude to teachers at school then no, I wouldn't bash him.
> *(Rory, aged 15)*

Therefore low level physical punishment was thought to be necessary for younger ages, but talking more appropriate for the older ones, except where the wrongdoing was serious, such as breaking windows, stealing or mugging.

Some young people spoke of preferring to receive a slap than the non-physical punishment that they actually got. Ewan spoke from his experience of preferring to be hit and get the punishment over with, rather than being locked away in his room:

> It wouldn't really work because I've been locked in my room
> sometimes and it's not really worked for me. But whenever
> I've been just smacked or just hit across the head it's actually
> worked because I know what I've done.
> *(Ewan, aged 13)*

And Paula's parents also grounded her if she did something wrong. She would have much preferred a quick physical punishment than a period of not being allowed out:

> Sometimes I get grounded for doing something wrong at
> school. I go 'I wish you'd rather hit me that ground me' – it
> would be better like that.
> *(Paula, aged 15)*

But while Paula was looking to be hit as a shorter punishment, Orla, from Northern Ireland, would have preferred being hit because she felt she deserved it if she'd been bad, and thought that the guilt she would feel if she was not so punished, was worse than the punishment itself.

> If I was hit I wouldn't do it again because I wouldn't want to
> get hit again. I'd rather my mammy whipped me, but
> sometimes they don't because then you always feel wile
> guilty, you know, as if you let her down or something and
> she's mad at me.
> *(Orla, aged 16)*

The young people could distinguish between what they saw as acceptable violence and what they saw as 'abuse'. They saw excessive violence, such as beating or 'battering' as abuse, and Jacquie for example, also cited hitting without reason:

> They have the right to hit their children if their children are
> bad or something like that, you just can't let them off with
> anything, but if you're hitting them for no reason, I think
> that's abuse – they don't have the right to do that.
> *(Jacquie, aged 12)*

For Pauline, abuse was hitting children all the time:

> …they shouldn't hit them all the time because that would be
> like abusing them. They should have the right to – if they do
> something wrong, like hit them, but not like really batter them.
> *(Pauline, aged 13)*

What level of physical punishment from parents can be deemed 'acceptable'
was clearly the subject of some contention, but the unacceptability of levels of
violence that become abusive was agreed. By condoning the use of even a
minimum of physical punishment the young people are accepting this as part of
the moral authority of parents, as well as being legitimate in teaching children,
often seen as those younger than themselves, what was right and wrong. The
general level of violence seen in a community also often reflects the level of
domestic violence. This may also be related to the social class characteristics of
an area in that although it is a generalisation, it has been suggested that it is the
middle class who tend to use less physical and more verbal methods of
discipline (or withdrawal of affection), while a more physical approach is more
characteristic of the working class.

But despite the discussion of acceptable or necessary physical punishment,
clearly not all the young people were advocates of punishments of this kind.
Those against it considered that parents failed to gain respect from their
children through hitting them, and accordingly, Maeve for example, was against
any sort of hitting of children, at any age:

> I've never been hit, but I definitely would NEVER use
> corporal punishment on a child, I really don't agree with
> that, so I wouldn't have that.
> *(Maeve, aged 14)*

Jack, aged 13, at school in the North of England, was also against it. His mother
did not use physical punishment, and he preferred her methods, which were to
withdraw his freedoms:

> But even if it's your mum she don't really have the right to
> hit you anyway 'cos you're only going to be bad again just to
> get back at her...It's not right for anyone to hit children 'cos
> it's cruel...And then like, my mum, she just like takes my
> spend away and things like grounds me, 'cos she, if I don't
> like being grounded I don't get into mischief, 'cos I don't
> want to be grounded.
> *(Jack)*

Some young people talked in terms of specific issues for which they felt some
kind of verbal parental guidance to be important, rather than just hitting them.
For example, Kiera and Tonya felt this was not appropriate for young people
caught smoking or drinking:

> **Kiera:** If your friend was caught smoking or drinking and
> they say to you – don't be doing that. If they found out you
> done it they shouldn't really give them a hiding and ground
> them for a while. They should talk to them about it and tell
> them what it's doing to their bodies and all.
> **Interviewer:** What do you think really works?
> **Tonya:** If they just sit down and talk to you, you come
> around.
> **Kiera:** Hitting you and stuff that's going to make you hate
> them and do it more.
> *(12–13-year-olds)*

Overall there was a moral sense from the Respect young people that if a child
behaves badly, there has to be some kind of punishment. As Guy asserted, 'If
you've been bad you've got to always have to have some kind of penalty, haven't
you?' A significant number supported some kind of physical admonishment, like
a smack or slap, while others preferred talking, reasoning and negotiation, or
deprivation of freedom or privileges. Comparing their views with those of the
much younger children (four to seven years) in Willow and Hyder's research
(1999) there seems to have been a shift in attitudes as young people become
more physically and emotionally competent and thereby more morally
independent. But does it also mean that they are already growing into adults who
condone a slap or even more? Are they taking an adult position, or their parent's
position on this? The contradiction is that although many can see that talking
and negotiation is better than hitting, they still tend to endorse a punitive moral
stand. In a follow-on study involving some of the Respect young people, they

described their memories of parental punishment for various wrongdoings when they were young, including smacking (Thomson and others 2003).

There was some diversity in opinions on how far parents should have the right to hit their own children, and to what extent, but overall it was felt that they did have some moral right.

> I expect my parents to slap me and shout at me but I don't
> expect my teachers or any other adults to do that.
> *(Lee, aged 14)*

It was absolutely clear that other adults, and particularly those outside the family, did not have this right at any level. This included neighbours, friends of parents, and definitely teachers, although in any case, corporal punishment is generally not allowed in schools today. Elliott and Gus had strong views on this:

> **Elliott:** And most of the kids like nowadays they're not used to
> it so if someone suddenly came out with a cane they would just
> get so shocked, man, they would be good for the rest of their
> lives! But you're not going to like the teacher are you?
> **Gus:** No teacher's going to push me around.
> *(13–14-year-olds)*

The unwritten rules of violence at home

Between siblings

> **Interviewer:** Are there any situations when you think
> violence does work?
> **Emma:** Your brother.
> **Interviewer:** What's different about that kind of violence?
> **Ella:** It's not violence, it's not like –
> **Emma:** It's what you're meant to do. Your brothers and sister
> are always fighting. That's about it.
> **Ella:** You sit down and you try and talk but they don't leave
> you alone so you have to hit them then.
> *(15–16-year-olds)*

In young people's eyes, fighting and violence between siblings, whether of the same sex or opposite sex, was a different moral issue. Whereas it is seen as wrong that violence occurs from a relatively more powerful parent to a child, and from a man to his female partner, the power equation is less obvious between siblings. The assumption is more of a mutual equality. This of course is not always true, as big brothers/sisters can beat up smaller ones, yet it is nevertheless far more acceptable to have fights between them. As Emma (above) commented, 'it's what you're meant to do'. Like violence between parents or against children is sometimes overlooked because it is 'in the family', this is also the case with brother and sister violence. It is something that is common in most families, and antagonism between siblings is looked on differently than that between unrelated people.

> **Aideen:** Big houses, like with big families, there's a wile lot of fights in them – but big families lead to big fights. Big sisters and brothers is always fighting like…
> **Roma:** I know – you beat the crap out of your wee sister, then your Dad hits you, then…But everyone does it to their cousins and all that – and little brothers.

In researching girls and violence, Burman, Brown and Batchelor (2003) also found that physical violence between siblings was not seen as 'violent', even if it was intended to cause physical harm, as such fights were normalised within the context of domestic and family relationships.

Yet this sibling/peer violence within the family may provide a practice ground for violence in the present or future outside the home. Kerby, aged 16, for instance, whose fighting activities are described in Chapter 4, was often beaten up by his cousins and said that this then became normal behaviour for him.

Between parents (or carers)

> Like married couples – you always see the husband battering the wife – you very rarely see the wife battering the husband.
> *(Bernadette, aged 13)*

Violence is a gendered behaviour. As Bernadette observed, it tends to be accepted knowledge that it is more usual for men to hit women in a relationship, than the reverse. Although there is occasionally some evidence of 'battered husbands', these are definitely a minority. While clearly there are various kinds of masculinities available to men, toughness and physical aggression is a traditional and working-class expression of masculinity, although by no means is domestic violence confined to the working class. Violence and drinking frequently coincide, and in the Respect study, several young people referred to fathers who were violent after they had been drinking, sometimes to their mother and sometimes to themselves as children. This had been the case for Devon, who was part of the gay and lesbian focus group, and who had moved out of his family home some time before. His father had always come home drunk and it was Devon and his siblings who had suffered:

> …when we was growing up he was always like that and when he did have work he just used to spend it over the pub, which we now know would sort of influence why he would treat us – you know, at the time we didn't know – because it's so natural for Dad to come in drunk and banging into the doorway and things, we just didn't think anymore of it. He'd come in most nights…and then he'd sort of yell at us, and very rarely he took it out on my mum, it was always us. I suppose because he was scared of my mum. My mum could hit back and we couldn't. We were just like four, five, you know…
> *(Devon, aged 17)*

Paul's father was also guilty of hitting his son, but attempted to dress it up as a sign of affection:

> Like my dad says – of a night, he goes, 'You know what, Paul?' He was drunk. I said 'What?' He goes, 'When I hit you it means that I love you.' And then I woke up the next morning and my mum goes, 'You remember what your dad said last night?', and I go, 'Yeah', and he goes, 'So when you get older you've got to hit your girlfriend, like it's a sign of loving someone.'
> *(Paul, aged 13)*

Bronagh, aged 14, spoke about the cruelty of men hitting their wives, and was afraid when her father used to physically abuse her mother:

> Abusing wives you know, men abusing wives. That's really
> cruel. You know, like, they're scared of the man, but they're
> just – it's really bad I think, really cruel to the woman. And
> they're all bruises and all, and they can't, they have to stay in
> the house all the time, in case anybody knows that their
> husband's beating them up or something like that
> there…My mum and my father, 'cos he used, you know, hit
> her all the time and I was scared.
> *(Bronagh)*

Location is a relevant factor here and in certain areas violence is common
currency, and there is a relationship between this wider culture of violence, and
domestic violence, and children grow up accommodating this.

However, there appears to be a contradiction in this gendered knowledge in
that it is common knowledge that men can and do hit women in a domestic
partnership, and yet many young men see it as generally unacceptable to hit
girls. Therefore there is some discrepancy in adolescent and adult masculinity
in terms of hitting girls or women. Young people are usually taught within the
family that boys should not hit girls (even though girls sometimes hit boys), and
yet this is not applied to husbands and wives. This group of 12–13-year-olds from
London observed how the 'rules' say that the boys cannot hit the girls back, at
least not until they are older:

> **Harry:** Well there's like ten girls, yeah? And they're all
> whacking you up – the worst you can do is shove them off,
> 'cos you can't whack them in the face.
> **Ismail:** And when you grow up and you'll have to fight back
> – but you can't fight girls back – you have to stick to that
> rule.
> **Trevor:** If like the woman's hitting you and you're going to
> hit her, yeah, she might just put out the knife and stab you!
> (laughter)
> **Shirleen:** Men don't hit women in the face till they get older.

Violence from children to parents

When children get older, they are often as big as their parents and therefore are as capable of inflicting harm on their parents as vice versa. Yet the 'rules' are more often in place that children do not hit their parents, particularly their mothers, and this tends to extend into adulthood. For Kerby, aged 16, it was his mother who brought him up, and although she might still try to hit him, he could not condone being violent back:

> …Mum's very strict…when you get on her bad side, you just don't wanna be on that side of her because even if I do something about it, she don't like it, she'll still try and hit me even though I'm well bigger than my mum. Much bigger than her but she'll still try and hit me and I can't do that so I just stand there and take it…She could do whatever she wants, I'd never hit her back. I've got too much respect for my parents to hit them back. Don't know how those kids can hit their mums after all they do for them.
> *(Kerby, aged 16)*

But somehow this rule changes in adult relationships, and is probably linked to the physical and marital power relationship that has historically underlined the marriage relationship. In some cultures, husbands have had a moral or even legal right to hit their wives, and in earlier centuries in Britain, a wife (as well as the children) was seen as the property of her husband and therefore he could dispense whatever treatment he chose. This is obviously no longer the case, but within the confined privacy of some homes, this abuse still goes on.

Cycles of violence

> Sometimes you get hit too much and whenever you're older and have wains of your own you hit them as well.
> *(Keith, aged 15)*

> If the parents are fighting all the time and the children see it, then it wouldn't be a good influence on them. They'd think it's something that parents do, but it's not, most of the time it's not.
> *(Rosa, aged 13)*

It is generally agreed that a child's upbringing has a great influence on their development, and this can clearly include a propensity to violence. The way a child is disciplined, and the amount of physical punishment this involves, can have implications for the sort of person they grow up into, and for the ways they treat others. It is well accepted that violence leads to further violence, and this can be the case in generational terms. A person who has experienced violence while growing up is more likely than others to repeat this in their own future family. In their study on bullying, Katz, Buchanan and Bream (2001) found that both bullies and victims revealed experiences of physical punishment and violence in the home and elsewhere, and it was these young people, but mainly the boys, who were significantly more likely to feel that it was acceptable to use violence to discipline a child. Cycles of violence may be perpetuated in this way, and these may be hard to break. The young people in the Respect study were aware of the risk of developing such a pattern, and a significant number of them, like Jodie, from the North of England, considered that being hit when they were children would make them think that this was normal behaviour to do to their own children:

> But when you've got like you're at home and like say parents
> say they've got to be strict by hitting you but if they hit you
> that just means you're going to hit some other people when
> you're older or you'll hit your children and it's not right.
> 'Cos if your parents hit you then you think it's right to go
> around hitting.
> *(Jodie, aged 13)*

The young people thought that if parents showed a bad example as role models, they would encourage this behaviour in their own children, and this violence could also escalate to partners as well as children:

> It's like, you know like if you're young and you see your mum
> and dad fight and argue and they like start hitting each other,
> when you grow up you'll think that's the right thing to do –
> start hitting your mum and dad, start hitting your wife.
> *(Matt, aged 13)*

A few who did reveal past childhood violence were able to make the connection between this and their own subsequent violence, which exemplified this cycle. Vanessa, now aged 17, who had been in care and fostered, had had bad experiences and grew up being quite violent herself:

> My mother's death had been a major impact in my life,
> which has really messed me up and then I got well violent
> because I got beaten up by foster parents for four years, and
> I was four – it was happening from four till eight, so I
> thought that was the way to be and it's just been going from
> bad to worse.
> *(Vanessa)*

It is not inevitable that children who have experienced violence at home will
always grow up into violent adults. Owen described his father as one who broke
from this mould:

> Yeah, 'cos I've seen both sides – when my dad was little he
> used to get punched by my grandad – he used to get
> punched straight into the face and he'd see stars and
> everything and my dad went – my dad could have gone to
> his sons – 'Right, I'm treating my kids like that', but he
> didn't, my dad went 'No, I'm not treating him like that, I'm
> going this way, I'm going to do it differently', and it's a
> better way.
> *(Owen, aged 16)*

Overall, the Respect young people generally saw parents as having a moral and
legitimate authority to physically chastise children within reason even though
they often preferred non-violent methods and were aware of the possibility of a
developing cycle of violence.

Key points

1. The views of the Respect young people, aged 11–17, who advocated some
   level of physical punishment contrasted with the views of younger children
   on smacking (Willow and Hyder 1999). If positive, non-violent discipline is
   to be promoted, these already formed views on an apparent 'moral' need for
   slapping or hitting as a punishment should be addressed.
2. The young people differentiated between what was acceptable and
   unacceptable levels of violence, that is, a slap was acceptable but beating or
   battering was not.

3. Some violence was seen as legitimised through being within the family, that is, parents and siblings could use some violence in their relationships with the young people but not others such as teachers, neighbours, or the police.

4. There are some gender contradictions between the morality of adolescent and adult violence, for example, boys are taught in the family and elsewhere that they should not hit girls, yet a level of violence in the family between men against women, appears to be accepted if not acceptable.

3 Bullying

> Everybody bullies everyone at some point don't they, there's loads of bullies.
>
> *(Tanya, aged 14)*

> To be rough you have to get rough. So going about here, getting slapped by everybody and all, you're getting rough. You have to learn to stand up for yourself, you can't always have back-up.
>
> *(Luke, aged 14)*

Everyone would condemn bullying while also acknowledging that it is widespread and has been so for a long time. It can be a problem at any age, and in a variety of environments, but it can be particularly prevalent in the school years when young people are congregated together. It has proved a more recent focus for scrutiny and research, for example, Rigby (2002) and Smith (2000). A study in 25 secondary schools by Glover and others (2000) showed that in any year 75 per cent of pupils were bullied, and 7 per cent of pupils were likely to experience severe and repeated bullying.

What children mean by 'bullying' can vary a lot. Research has shown that definitions may vary between repeated physical or verbal actions to 'anything that someone does that is nasty and hurts me' (Swain 1998). Rigby (2002) has produced a definition which suggests that bullying 'involves a desire to hurt + hurtful action + a power in-balance + (typically) repetition + an unjust use of power + evident enjoyment by the aggressor and generally a sense of being oppressed on the part of the victim'. Social exclusion by peers can also be seen as a form of bullying. Children themselves are very aware of these kinds of possibilities, whether in their own lives or those of other children. Bullying can happen inside and outside school and much has been written describing the problem and making practical suggestions, such as that by Oliver and Candappa (2003). A comprehensive study by Katz, Buchanan and Bream (2001) looked at the extent of bullying in children and adolescents in Britain both in and out of school and presented their views and experiences. They found more than one in ten had experienced severe bullying and almost all children had had experienced some type of bullying including name-calling. In 2001, when the Office of Children's Rights Commissioner for London (OCRCL) conducted a survey on the views of children and young people about living in London, bullying was the fourth most cited issue that they felt that people in authority in London should take action on (Sharpe 2002a). They wrote comments and their own suggestions on what they thought could be done about it, from severely punishing the bullies to having security guards and CCTV at school.

Bullying was also an issue that the Respect young people had opinions on, and in some cases, personal experience. They all recognised 'bullying', although their personal definitions may have differed. It was bullying by peers that was their main concern, and adult–child bullying was not discussed. In the questionnaire they were asked to give their judgements on 'bullying'. Overall, 80 per cent asserted that bullying was 'always wrong', and another 12 per cent that it was 'usually wrong'. Bullying also came up in their cited dilemmas, the proportion increasing for the younger age groups. It peaked as a concern in Years 7 and 8, when young people are about 11–13 years, to be at least partly replaced in the later years by dilemmas about drugs, alcohol, and under-age sex.

In this chapter, the Respect young people discuss the nature and experience of bullying and bullies, and their own advice on how to respond to bullies. In the focus groups, one of the contentious statements discussed was 'Being bullied toughens you up'. This produced lively discussion, in which the consensus was to disagree, but some of the contradictions expressed suggested that in this and in other aspects of bullying, the issue is certainly not a straightforward one.

Who gets bullied, and how?

> It depends, if you've got no friends, or if they're a bit ugly…
> *(Ali, aged 15)*

There were a number of things that seemed to set off bullying behaviour. It is easy to suggest that it is because bullied people are different in some way, but clearly not all people who are different are bullied so there must be a combination of personal, social and environmental aspects that make a person more vulnerable to bullying. The Respect young people did describe people who are bullied as generally 'different', for instance, because of their race, religion, size, sexuality, etc., as Lucy observed:

> I've never actually got slagged off, but I do know some
> people who have got slagged off for being overweight, for
> being not nice looking, for having a bad personality and
> everything and I know one that fits all three of them, out of
> our class. It's not really fair to be going around slagging
> them either for it, you know, they can't help it.
> *(Lucy, aged 14)*

Steven, aged 14, who himself lived within a disadvantaged area in the North of England, observed that some children are the subjects of bullying simply because they are poor and their families could not afford decent clothes:

> This kid, in Year 7 or 8, gets a lot of stick too, because he's
> got no clothes and that. He gets a lot of bullying, off the
> people in our school…but he manages to keep a brave face
> on, you know, he comes into school every day. He's not
> being beaten by the bullies. (But) I think he will break
> sometime – he'll stop coming in, yeah, he'll start wagging it
> and that.
> *(Steven)*

Disability is a 'difference' that may be more likely to evoke bullying than other differences (Rigby 2002). It often seems to occur even though the people who verbally tease or abuse know that this is wrong and unfair. Elliott commented on two other boys in his year who got bullied, one because of his disability, and the other because he was not clean:

> Like Matthew and Simon, they just get bullied all the time.
> Matthew's got learning difficulties and if a teacher lets him
> off a bit, people will go mad about that, and Simon, he's
> quite dirty, skin dirty and stuff, I dunno, there's just certain
> people that…because people don't like them.
> *(Elliott, aged 13)*

As Rigby and others suggest, bullying often involves a power relationship, in that bullies clearly like to and need to pick on people who are weaker than themselves, as endorsed by Jack and his friends, aged 12–13, living in the North of England:

> **Jack:** If you're bullying you're going to pick on someone that you know won't touch you…and say like – like you come to someone stronger than you – if you start bullying them you'll get beat up…
> **Guy:** Yeah, like one day, there's always someone bigger than you and harder than you.
> **Jack:** And better than you!

Aspects of race and ethnicity are also often triggers for bullying. In the OCRCL survey, over half of those who expressed their main concern with bullying came from cultural backgrounds that were other than 'white English' (Sharpe 2002a). In the study by Katz, Buchanan and Bream (2001) a quarter of the minority children were severely bullied compared to 13 per cent of 'white' children. Interestingly, in one Respect focus group of 14–15-year-old young women from the rural school, where there were few children from cultures other than 'white', they appeared to choose an ethnic group to pick on as they might choose some kind of fashion:

> **Rosie:** It would go in fashions almost –
> **Yvette:** They'd choose somebody to pick on and if there was something they could pick on they would use it…Yeah, it's like sometimes started off by like one person – 'cos you know Alex got a lot of stick from one of the girls a couple of years lower than us who was sort of calling her Paki and all of a sudden it was like half the girls in that year picked it up, whereas it had never been a problem before. 'Cos like everyone else in the school was white, there wasn't anybody else at the time.
> **Rosie:** And suddenly it would be a fashion not to like Paki – if anyone did they would be looked down upon, so it was like some people would find it very confusing 'cos they could be a bit behind. (laughter)

Those who are victims of bullying do not seem to be 'chosen' for consistent reasons, they may not be 'different', but they do seem to be vulnerable to being bullied at the particular time or situation. It is significant that Katz, Buchanan and Bream found that both bullies and bullied had experienced physical punishment inside and outside the home.

Although bullying may be physical, the most frequently mentioned aspect of bullying by the Respect young people was 'slagging', meaning the use of verbal abuse or insults, about some aspect of the person being bullied, or a member of their family. Both Ken and Shannon, at school in Northern Ireland, described this kind of abuse:

> Slagging off people's parents and stuff like that. Slagging is bullying. Calling people names is bullying…people have been up in the office crying.
> *(Ken, aged 14)*

> …but they put you down, they just put down about everything…sometimes at the clothes you wear, they slag about, or your shoes, or the size of your feet, the way you're made, your eyes, your hair, they slag you about things, your teeth and braces, all of it.
> *(Shannon, aged 13)*

In talking about the nature of bullying, some of the Respect young people spoke about their own experiences of being bullied, and the gender differences involved. The young people also suggested that boys' bullying might be more open, in the public sphere, whereas girls' bullying may be more private and hidden. Jacqueline, aged 15, who grew up in a rural village, had to endure bullying for four years of her school life. This bullying was insidious in that the female bully did not have to touch her or even need to speak to make her life almost unbearable:

> I wouldn't call it bullying as such, just making someone's life complete hell for four years. It wasn't really bad like, it was just like words, it wasn't anything else but words, but I don't really remember much, I tried to shut it out but she used to, oh I don't know what she used to do, she just used to come up and stare and just not say anything and then go away and laugh.
> *(Jacqueline)*

Jacqueline's experience was a kind of social exclusion, a bullying by demoralisation. This kind of bullying is more characteristic of girls than boys, whereby girls use more verbal or passive means such as blackmailing, name-calling, exclusion and racism (Katz, Buchanan and Bream 2001). Boys tend to bully more than girls, and do it more physically or directly, and although boys may bully other boys, and also girls, it is less likely that girls bully boys (Rigby 2002). For Judy, aged 12, her earlier experience of being bullied by other girls sent her more into the company of boys, which she still preferred:

> ...I've always got along better with boys because girls used to
> bully me when I was younger...they just used to be really
> horrible so I just used to go off and muck around with the
> boys and play football and things. I used to get lots of names
> and things, so now, I probably get on better with boys than
> I do with girls, but then again I do get on with girls.
> **(Judy)**

Katz, Buchanan and Bream (2001) also observed that male bullies and bullied boys live by the myths of traditional masculinity that involve images of toughness and a physical notion of maleness. Nevertheless, verbal bullying is the most frequent form, and although it is usually more physically larger and more powerful people who bully, they do not necessarily achieve this through physical means.

What about the bullies?

> Bullies probably bully people because they feel as if they're
> stronger and all like.
> **(Pauline, aged 13)**

> But it all depends – sometimes bullies are really soft inside
> but they're just acting hard to get the attention.
> **(Judy, aged 12)**

Some of the young people questioned why bullies behave the way they do. While Pauline (above) thought it was to feel stronger and more powerful, in Shannon's view, the fact that certain people bully others indicated the low levels of their own self-esteem:

> Some of the girls that are the fighters, the people who are
> the leaders or whatever, they are the ones who would
> actually put you down. I think it's a sign of their insecurity
> actually, they don't think highly of themselves if they have to
> slag another person.
> *(Shannon, aged 13)*

Those who have considered this question (such as Rigby 2002) are still left
somewhat puzzled as to what the bullies really get out of it, and the study by
Katz, Buchanan and Bream(2001) suggests that bullies come from all types of
families. The Respect young people had little sympathy for the bullies, and did
not spend much time pondering the reasons they bullied, but they did talk
about respect, and the question of whether or not bullying people could
produce respect or admiration in others for the bully. The views were mixed,
but the balance was probably negative, that bullying does not gain respect for
the bully. This was the view of 15-year-old Rory, living in London:

> Say if Anthony's the local bully yeah, I ain't going to respect
> him for being a bully. If I saw him bashing someone younger
> than him and I felt sorry for the other person I'm going to
> have a go at him, ain't I? So no mate, it don't bring respect
> you know, thinking you are a hard nut and a bully.
> *(Rory)*

Yet clearly some young people could see bullying in certain contexts as earning
respect, but this is mixed up with fear (see also Chapter 4).

> If you're in school, right, and you see this wee boy every day
> and you start punching him, every day of the week, he's
> going to start respecting you because he's scared of you.
> *(Bernadette, aged 13)*

But where fear does produce a form of respect, it is a negative form, and
different from the respect that people can feel for others who have a much
more 'honourable' type of behaviour.

In the Home Counties, 15-year-old Edward also agreed that fear could be a form of
respect and it is this sort of 'respect' that he thought bullies are after. He suggested
that it is the person who beats a bully who would get more respect, and thus
violence used in this 'moral' way gets respect, while a bully's violence does not:

> If someone was getting beaten up and you stop it using
> violence then they'll respect you, they'll think you're kind to
> them, they'll admire you, whereas if you're the bully then
> they'll hate you and you won't get respect by using violence.
> *(Edward)*

Judy denounced bullies and their admirers, but she was aware that some people
in school courted attention and thereby some popularity through being
'horrible', a tactic with which she totally disagreed:

> People who admire bullies are not very nice. I don't admire
> bullies. If someone's got you by the scruff of the neck and
> they say 'Give me your lunch money' or something, that's
> not respect, that's just being horrible, and they mostly do it
> for attention, for people to go, 'Oh my god, he's so strong',
> or 'Oh my god, how could she do that to someone', or
> 'She's got so much confidence', or something. But you don't
> have to be horrible to be good. You don't have to be
> horrible to be admired.
> *(Judy, aged 12)*

Overall, the young people condemned bullying, and bullies, although some
gave grudging acknowledgement that this could produce admiration and even
popularity.

Effects of bullying

> I think it made me stronger than I already was, well I can
> now deal with anything, I mean I did cry, she did make me
> cry a couple of times because it got really bad, but I got
> totally sick of it, and really tired, you know, it made me
> tired…it's all over now.
> *(Jacqueline, aged 15)*

The children and young people in London participating in the OCRCL survey
who chose bullying as their main issue for action, saw many dire effects resulting
from bullying, from anxiety, loss of confidence, missing school, to illness,
running away, and even suicide (Sharpe 2002a), and this has been documented
elsewhere (Borg 1998, Elliott 2002). The Department of Education and

Employment estimated that about a third of girls and a quarter of boys are afraid to go to school at some time because of bullying (DfEE 1999). The young people in the Respect project also described possible bad effects of bullying, and spoke of similar consequences. But there was some support for the idea that being bullied could serve to toughen up the individual, as though it was a kind of character-building experience. This was also a suggestion considered, and rejected, by Rigby (2002). In relation to this, one of the contentious statements discussed in some of the focus groups was 'Being bullied toughens you up' and this produced a mixture of views. Some allowed the possibility that persistent bullying or even beatings could somehow strengthen the person, which they saw as a possible protective device. For example, Seamus, aged 13, from Northern Ireland, believed if you ignore the bully, he would think you are afraid of him, and therefore it will make you stronger if you stand up to him:

> If anybody is bullying you in the street it would toughen you
> up just to, hit them'uns too in the street instead of walking
> away from them and letting them know you're afraid of them.
> It toughens you up, aye, instead of walking away from
> somebody you're afraid of, just turn round and hit them back.
> *(Seamus)*

Some suggested it could 'firm up' a person as they got used to being bullied. This way they could perhaps escape violence by hiding its effects. Aaron, living in the North of England, was a young man who had been subjected to homophobic bullying, and he agreed that not fighting back had made him stronger:

> (I've been bullied) yeah, daily, every day, but I think it makes
> me stronger as well. I would never stand and bite back, you
> know, I just take it in. It's not nice, it's not nice immediately,
> but if you look forward and think how much it's built on
> your character then I think it could be OK.
> *(Aaron, aged 16)*

Ali, aged 15, who was in a Pupil Referral Unit, spoke from the role of having been a bully himself. He knew what it was like to bully someone, and he believed that it could make them 'kinda strong', which helped him to rationalise his behaviour:

> I see other people getting bullied and you get kinda strong,
> they get kinda braced, 'cos they get used to the
> beatings…they just firm up 'cos they're used to it aren't they.
> It's an everyday thing…
> *(Ali)*

But this group of 15-year-old boys, also at this Unit, could not see any positive effects of bullying, quite the contrary:

> **Interviewer:** So have you seen people getting stronger and
> tougher as they've been bullied?
> **Perry:** No.
> **Adam:** They go all weak. (laughs)
> **Perry:** It f***s up their heads man, continuously getting
> beaten up every day. It f***s up your brain…If they start
> getting brave, they just get it worse!…Some people that get
> bullied f******* kill themselves.

Although being bullied may seem to make a person 'harder' in some ways (Thomson 2000a), this is not a positive way of gaining inner strength, but more a strategy of rationalising what is happening. If someone has been bullied, and was offered the time over again, it is extremely unlikely that they would repeat the bullying in order to get 'stronger'.

Advice from young people

Stand up for yourself

> If say you get bullied, bullies are just cowards, but if you stick
> up for yourself, if you stand up to the bully, they'll never do
> it again 'cos they're the cowards – like if you prove that
> you're not as coward as they are then they'll leave you
> alone…I think it probably does give you more self-
> confidence if you stick up for yourself.
> *(Estelle, aged 14)*

> Yeah, but if you carry on being bullied and you don't stick up
> for yourself you're going to lose all the confidence you have.
> *(Sandie, aged 15)*

The most popular action prescribed for those being bullied to toughen them up was to stand up to the bullying, rather than 'taking it', as Estelle and Sandie advised above. 'Standing up for yourself' was a familiar theme in young people talking about violence at school and in the community, as seen in later chapters. But it is a moral imperative that is easier said than done, and many victims of bullying would testify to this, however effective it can prove to be. Ali (quoted earlier) in his experience as a bully, thought that bullying started being 'boring' if the victim started standing up for themselves. But if the bully saw it was hurting someone, he would do it all the more:

> [bullying] won't hurt them will it, and if they think it ain't hurting them so they leave them, 'cos they get bored with them. When you beat someone and they start crying it's like funny, you think 'yeah, they're crying so it's hurting them', so you carry on. If you beat someone up and they just get up and walk off and – it's boring you know what I mean – if they start standing up for themselves…
> *(Ali, aged 15)*

Ali goes on to almost imply that his bullying has done someone a favour. There are contradictions in his own account that illustrate the complexity of the process, while his matter-of-fact style makes bullying sound like a normal fact of life:

> When I first bullied him like he was like weak, but everyone bullies him now like he just stands up to you – and you think, 'aah, I'll leave you'. And he stands up to everyone else and no-one bullies him no more, just swear at him stuff like that…If you beat someone and you take their money from them, then you carry on, 'cos you know you get their money. If they don't give it to you then you go and find someone else…Some people I knew in my last school got bullied and they just carry on with their life, they don't care.
> *(Ali)*

The psychological discourse around bullying that young people engage in assumes that there are such strategies that others should adopt to confront this behaviour. There was no shortage of views asserting that people should stand up for themselves if they get bullied, on the basis that if the bully realises that he or she is effective, they will do it even more.

> See if you're going somewhere and they say something to
> you and you show fear like, you know they're going to pick
> on you again so you have to do something about it. If you do
> something about it they won't do it again.
> *(Eoghan, aged 13)*

Finding the strength and confidence to do this may not be easy but some young
people implied that they had found this within themselves, or through the
support of someone close, like Della, now 17, and Lauren, aged 14:

> In the state school I went to there were a group of girls in
> my year who liked to be in charge of everyone and if a new
> person came along they'd start on them and make them well
> aware that they were hard and they were to be stayed well
> clear of…I mean I got myself into trouble in the first four
> weeks at the school because I ended up having a fight with
> one of the girls, but I mean one thing is, they never actually
> bothered me again, so…and then a lot of people respected
> me for doing that and then that's how I got – made a lot of
> friends.
> *(Della)*

> They'd always call me fat and everything and I wouldn't eat,
> and then just started eating 'cos me Nana said just take
> yourself for who you are, it's like back to me Nana again…if
> people don't like you then they don't like you, all your
> family loves you and your friends and everything, so…like
> now I stick up for meself, but I won't go round starting fights
> or anything. If they give me dirty looks, or instead of going
> up being gobby I say why are you giving me dirty looks and
> have you got summat against me and people like instead of
> going up and being gobby they'll talk it through with me.
> *(Lauren)*

Elsa, a young woman with a rather acerbic manner and a level of attitude that
cared little of what others thought of her, was confident in her verbal skills and
it would be unlikely that she would be such a victim:

> If I was bullied, I wouldn't tell the teacher, I think I'd just
> make sure they wouldn't do it again, not like beating them
> up or killing them or anything, you know, just coming out
> with something really, really sort of good to shut them up,
> you know, there's always a good way.
> *(Elsa, aged 14)*

Francis, aged 16, also advocated the use of verbal rather than physical responses to bullying, especially for those like himself, who were not 'physical' people:

> Well, you can always use a verbal, but you've got to be
> cunning – 'cos I'm not sort of particularly physical myself so
> I have to be more verbal if I get threatened, and just use
> comments and stuff to try and embarrass them and things.
> *(Francis, aged 16)*

If there is any respect to be gained from a bullying situation, it does probably come from a person standing up for themselves by physical or verbal means. But doing so requires the presence of a certain level of confidence, and if that is absent, a bullied person may feel ashamed that they are not capable of any resistance, and this makes it even harder to admit to someone that it is happening or do anything about it:

> It's hard. You don't want to look weak in front of them…if
> it's immature, stupid names and all that there, you'd just
> laugh and walk on. If it's something serious and hurtful you
> can't do it.
> *(Tina, aged 16)*

Ignoring the bully

Some young people recommended a more passive response to bullying which was to ignore it. This can have mixed results. Pascal, like Ali (quoted earlier), thought it would be effective because the bullying would became boring:

> Sometimes, say if they're giving you a hard time, you just
> ignore them and they'll just get bored with it and say – 'Hold
> on a minute, this isn't affecting him' – so they'll wise up.
> *(Pascal)*

Steven too, in the North of England, thought people should not get so upset about name-calling:

> I don't think you should really take names to heart 'cos you
> are what you are and you can't change it so what's the point
> in worrying about it…I think it is (easier to ignore being
> called names). I just look on them as being stupid. You've
> not got much of a life really if you've got to go round calling
> other people.
> *(Steven, aged 14)*

Edward, at school in the Home Counties, advised passive avoidance by ignoring the bullying:

> If somebody thinks you don't care then there is no point in
> them bullying you because most bullies do it to get respect
> and if you show contempt then that makes them more angry,
> but if you just ignore it, show them you couldn't care less,
> then they just walk away, try someone else – 'cos fear is a
> form of respect.
> *(Edward, aged 15)*

But it very much depends on the context and type of bullying and ignoring it can also make things worse. This response tactic is something easier said than done, especially if the bullies are saying or doing very hurtful things. This was Jacqueline's experience:

> I just ignored it and she hated it me ignoring her, it just
> made it worse so you just didn't know how to handle it
> because if I said anything to her that'd land me in trouble
> but if I ignored it, it made her stronger. So it's like, she,
> from all the advice like Mum gave me, it made her stronger,
> it made her thrive on it and made her do it more, but I
> didn't understand by ignoring her how she could get
> anything out of it if I wasn't reacting to it, but it made her
> do it more. I thought, 'Oh I'll ignore her she'll get sick of it
> but she never did.'
> *(Jacqueline, aged 15)*

Telling someone

> 'Cos I was getting bullied once by people in my class and I
> kept it in my head for ages and I didn't tell anyone, not even
> me friends, and 'cos it was one of me friends that was
> bullying me and I kept it and kept it in my head for ages and
> then just one day I come home and I just started crying in
> front of me mum 'cos it got too much so me mum come in
> and saw one of the teachers, but it's all over and done with
> now.
> *(Sarah, aged 12)*

In the Respect questionnaire, 80 per cent of the young people considered that
'telling the teacher you've been bullied' was 'rarely' or 'never wrong'. But this
does not reflect the low reporting of bullying by child victims to adults. In the
focus group discussions of these issues, it was clear that things were not so
straightforward. Various fears were raised, for example, that if you tell on a
bully, the bullying will get worse, or that it may increase so that others join in, or
that gangs may even get involved. Some young people were of the belief that by
not telling someone, by keeping it inside you, this may be self-strengthening
and does not give the bully the satisfaction of knowing that he or she is causing
pain and hurt. In certain situations, and with certain individuals, telling the
teacher, a parent, or another adult may sort out this problem, but in others it
can serve to escalate it.

The most obvious people to tell are parents or teachers, and this had worked
well for Pauline:

> I was bullied in the school by this girl…it was wile scary. She
> always used to keep going on and on and then you'd say to
> your mammy that you were sick so that you couldn't go to
> school. It would just go on and on and you couldn't really
> talk back or anything. But then the teachers in school were
> wile – really good and they sorted it out and she was
> suspended for a week and it hasn't happened since, but I
> have seen her doing it.
> *(Pauline, aged 13)*

But Kofi, in a group of 14- to 15-year-old young men in London, was not convinced
that teachers would necessarily be very effective in dealing with a bully:

> **Kofi:** Bullies get brought down in the end.
> **Interviewer:** Who brings bullies down?
> **Kofi:** The people that ain't scared of them.
> **Interviewer:** And who would that be?
> **Kofi:** Teachers can – some teachers can – some teachers can't. Some teachers don't, they just forget about it. Some teachers are scared of them bullies as well.

Amy, aged 13, who attended the school in the Home Counties, was aware that children and young people being bullied can feel afraid to tell anyone if the bullies are threatening to do something even worse if they do reveal it:

> Sometimes you think – oh, they're not going to listen to me, why should I tell them…And bullying comes in very many different forms so it really depends on what – but it's just – it's scary if you want to go and tell someone that you're being bullied and the bully can threaten you saying, if you tell on me then I'm going to do this to you or I'm going to do this to something that's very close to you – or something like that, so it does feel scary to tell.
> *(Amy)*

Elsa, from the same school, thought that although bullying was given high priority for action in this school, it was not worth telling teachers as this did not work in the long term:

> I think bullying does go on, but they take it really, really seriously here. It's like, if you give an evil look, then if someone tells the teacher you can get in a lot of trouble for it. They say you should always tell a teacher, but you're just gonna get bullied, if not by the same person or by different people, for doing it, and the teacher's done something about it, and it still goes on, it might stop for a little while, but they can't do a lot about it. They can suspend the person but they'll be back again, you know, in a week's time, still doing what they're doing.
> *(Elsa, aged 14)*

Elsa did not live in an area where there was a culture of violence. Tanya on the other hand, came from an inner-city estate where violence, including bullying, was common currency. She counselled fighting rather than talking, and certainly not telling a teacher:

> Yeah, I think (a fight does sort it out), not talking, 'cos if
> you talk, they just think, well, she's scared of me. Telling
> somebody, that even makes it worse, like telling the teachers,
> that makes it worse. 'Cos if I just told the teacher I was
> getting bullied and that it's this person, they wouldn't stop
> it, they'd still bully you more. It's like that. They don't listen
> to the teachers anyway.
> *(Tanya, aged 14)*

When asked elsewhere in the questionnaire to say if and when it was OK to tell on
someone, 13 per cent of the Respect young people gave bullying as a justification.
But there is a strong taboo against telling or 'grassing' (Mellor 1999). This response
was made more often by the younger age groups, and by those living in England
more often than those in Northern Ireland. In the same area and school, Kay and
Naomi discussed the perils of 'grassing' on other people in their class:

> **Kay:** If they're there all the time in your class, they're your
> mates but they're sort of like bullying you, calling you
> names, you can't really ignore it.
> **Naomi:** You don't like to grass on them do you – then they
> call you more and everything. It's quite hard to tell teachers
> when you're being bullied…and stuff then like if you grass
> they call you a grass and they call you more then, and then
> they get gangs on to you or something.
> **Interviewer:** And would it be easier for a friend to tell the
> teacher?
> **Kay:** Your friends would say you shouldn't be grassing up for
> your friends. It could make things worse because then they
> could start on your friend as well…there's not a lot teachers
> can do really, because it always happen like after school and
> everything.

It may depend on the actions and the personality of the teacher they tell:

> I'd say it all depends on the person you're telling – I mean
> I know Mrs P, she's quite easy to talk to if you want to tell
> something, but you know, then it's the whole school that
> knows about it…and if you're with someone who, someone
> who is going to linger around the problem, just going to
> keep saying, 'Oh just ignore them', then it's a lot harder.
> *(Judy, aged 12)*

Telling teachers can be a risk, trusting the formal authority of the school over the informal hierarchy. While some of these young people spoke positively of the need to tell someone like a teacher, others implied that it was sometimes better remaining private, and within the informal culture of the school. But this does not usually provide a solution unless the bullied person manages to adopt a successful strategy. Their experiences make it clear why so many bullied children phone helplines instead of telling parents or teachers.

Homophobic bullying

> Like say the boy found out what sexuality he was say he was gay, they would really slag him because I think in a way they're scared of their own sexuality, they don't even know what they are yet…it's just stupid things really, a lot of the things they slag people about. They just try to get off the subject of themselves, they don't want people to look at them.
> *(Shannon, aged 13)*

> **Interviewer:** Do you have any lesbians in class?
> **All:** Not that we know of.
> **Interviewer:** What would happen if there were?
> **Yasmin:** I suppose if everyone found out they'd be bullied.
> **Lorraine:** Yeah, they would be bullied.
> *(14–15-year-olds from London)*

Homophobic bullying is a particular form of bullying, based on the assumption of a person's sexuality, and is a common and recognised occurrence, especially in schools, as Shannon and the 14- to 15-year-olds quoted above illustrate. GALOP (1997) found that 82 per cent of gay men, lesbians and bisexuals surveyed had been verbally abused and 60 per cent reported being hit or kicked during their time at school. Homophobia among young people plays a major part in enforcing gender conformity, and thus to the construction of heterosexuality. It is often enacted within a same-sex group, a homosocial activity that contributes to confirming and enforcing a strongly heterosexual stance. Homophobia among boys is a well documented feature of school life, and Epstein (1996, 1997) has described how boys who did not behave in an 'appropriately' macho way were often victims of this form of sexism, expressed in terms of their supposed similarities to girls. High levels of homophobia emerged in the Respect focus groups and in some of the interviews, and reflected a need to be constantly enforcing or policing gender boundaries. It was partly another form of 'slagging', by calling into question a person's sexuality, by calling them gay, or lesbian, and some of the Respect young people suggested that this bullying could take more physical forms:

> **Interviewer:** What if someone was gay, you know, somebody at school, would it be safe for them to be open about it?
> **Tanya:** Bully them…
> **Sonia:** They'd batter them or something.
> **Donna:** And go like 'He's gay!'
> *(14–15-year-olds)*

> [Bullying] can be quite – some people act quite severe along with it, like if they find out people that are gay they'll go and hurt them and things like that, and tease them.
> *(Francis, aged 16)*

It was significant that in the Respect project the young women could talk quite easily about issues of homosexuality, and did so at some length, whereas the young men were very circumspect about it, as if simply discussing it could imply something about their own sexuality. The Respect young people's views on homosexuality are discussed in more detail by Sharpe (2002) and Sharpe and Thomson (forthcoming). For boys and young men, any association with femininity, which gayness has, can be experienced as a slur on their masculinity. It can be a most effective way of bullying, as many have found, and is a subject that badly needs addressing in sex and relationship lessons and school anti-bullying programmes.

Bullying is essentially indefensible. It is an unfair power relationship between someone who is acting with physical or verbal abuse against another person who is seen as different and weaker in some way and it may have severe consequences. The young people's discussion on bullying revealed layers of complexity and the various dilemmas involved in trying to do something about it. Like the problem, the possible courses of action are not simple, as the young people have described. For example, telling someone seems the obvious solution but it can backfire and worsen the situation. Teachers need to be vigilant but they also need to handle things in a tactful and delicate way. There did not seem to be a great deal of confidence from the young people that this would sort things out. Their own major recommendation was to stand up to the bully, but this takes a certain confidence, which may already be undermined. There has been quite of lot of research on bullying with the aim of setting up strategies to counter bullying, especially in schools, but it is still a perennial problem, and one that requires vigilance and sensitivity. What inhibits progress may be the nature of school culture by which the rigidity of educational authority is not open to participation (Cutler and Frost 2001), and creates a split between formal and informal school cultures so that interactions in either direction involve some kind of dramatic event. Greater participation or power-sharing with young people in schools may make this divide less polarised and ease communication. In this context, young people taking their own initiative against a bully represents a low level of participation in schools.

The potential for bullying inside and outside school is one of the infringements on personal safety experienced by children and young people today. This kind of behaviour provides a serious threat to the increased freedoms that young people are said to enjoy in contemporary society, and their rights to a safe environment.

Key points

1. Bullying is seen as morally wrong by a great majority. The young people were divided in whether a bully gained respect from his/her activities – some thought they did, and that they were admired for this kind of 'power', it made them 'popular' and people wanted to be their friends. But others (usually the older ones) were more aware that this was confusing respect and admiration with fear.
2. Although bullying is not seen as legitimate or justifiable, there was some support for the notion that being bullied could be character strengthening. This is a rationalisation by the bully, or by the bullied to try and define some worth from the experience, or a method of concealing the pain and hurt, and reflects another popular discourse on bullying.
3. Advice from many of the young people in response to bullying was to 'stand up for yourself'. But this depends on the type of person, and style of bullying. Even if they would do this, some young people simply do not know the best way to do so and are aware that it can backfire and make the bullying worse. In relation to 'standing up for yourself', many young people, particularly in the cultures of violence, considered that a fight was the way to sort things out quickly and effectively.

4. Telling that someone has been bullied is advised but many would hesitate to do this.

5. If some way could be found to lessen the divide between the formal and informal culture of the school through greater participation, then communication about bullying and strategies to deal with it might be facilitated.

6. Some suggest that a cycle of bullying may be set up and evidence shows that those who have received physical violence at home and elsewhere are more likely to bully others (Katz, Buchanan and Bream 2001).

4 Fighting

I wouldn't be, y'know, slagged 'cause everybody, you know,
kinda thinks that I'm one of the best fighters and that…but I
don't like fighting – I, I try and avoid fights most like I can,
never liked fighting, always hated it…most of them it was
kinda other people that started it and I would, I didn't like
people saying stuff about my dad like you know.
(Matthew, aged 13)

I mean, my mum says like when she was little she was always
taught not to fight, now girls they just scrap and scrap.
(Charlotte, aged 14)

Fighting was a subject that many of the Respect young people were familiar
with, as participants or observers. For some it was seen as a quick and effective
way to sort out a situation. It is hard to separate fighting, the use of physical
aggression against other people, from other related aspects of violence such as
bullying, and community violence, but this section focuses on the relationship
between fighting and self-defence, respect, defending others and family honour,
the role of friends, and some gendered aspects of fighting. It reflects the
meanings and significance of fighting in their lives. Fighting was mainly
discussed in the focus groups through the statements: 'Violence is the only way
to get respect', or 'Sometimes violence is the only way to get things done'. The
majority gave some qualified disagreement to these statements, and it was clear
that location was very relevant to the incidence, role, and views, of young people
related to fighting. If the young people lived in areas where there was a culture
of violence, although they may not approve of violence, nor think it necessarily
promoted respect for the perpetrators, it was nevertheless a fact of life. This was
the case, for example, in working-class areas of a Northern Irish city:

> There's a wile lot of fights now between teenagers…There's
> all wee ones been left in hospital, ones smashing bottles over
> each other's heads and all. And knives, they took knives up
> to discos and all that to each other, all over certain – 'cause
> of wee girls, she's going with somebody and they're afraid to
> talk to some other wee fella and all. Jesus, it's ridiculous.
> *(Aideen, aged 14)*

For those in the working-class Northern Ireland and North of England schools, fighting was viewed as a 'normal' activity, and this was often the case for both sexes. Northern Ireland has long been subject to the violence characterising sectarian feuds and the general level of antagonism between the two opposing religious groups was constantly high in certain areas, as described in Chapter 5. Those at school in the working-class estate in the North of England gave a mixture of views, and their agreement with statements endorsing violence rested on whether the violence was to protect members of the family, or family honour. Gangs were more important in this location, where these allowed individuals some protection from name-calling. In some situations and locations, fighting was more common in the younger age groups, and generally decreased with age as young people preferred to sort out conflict in other ways. But especially in areas where there were cultures of adult conflict and violence, and where there appeared to be more 'reasons' for violence, such as in retaliation for something done, the fighting did not abate in the same way.

Fighting and respect

> I don't think violence gets you respect, it just makes some
> people scared of you, and fear and respect are two totally
> different things…respect is when you look up to someone in
> a good way not in a negative way.
> *(Crystal, aged 16)*

> There is a few who are more respected than others, but
> that's because they can fight and people are scared of them,
> that's why they're respected, well, looked up to.
> *(Shannon, aged 13)*

One thing that young people are aware of, and value, is respect. In relation to violence and fighting, you may, for example, get respect for defending yourself, but violence itself does not automatically gain respect. It may result in fear, or the pretence of respect for security reasons. Yet, for some young people, being a 'good fighter' could bring them respect. It seemed to depend on how it was used. Thus, 'respect' for violence through fighting was morally qualified, according to how it is used, perhaps a bit like the morality of Robin Hood's activities. Fighting to defend someone who is being bullied gains respect; whereas unprovoked fighting, or physical bullying does not. But a disadvantage of being seen as a 'good fighter', like the gunfighters in Westerns, is that every other fighter wants to fight you, as David had found:

> It's better to keep yourself to yourself, because then you
> don't get in as much trouble…But if they know you,
> someone might come up to you and start trouble and then
> you may have to hit them or something like that…because
> when I went up, went from juniors, I had loads of fights and
> then everyone knew me because of my fighting and then
> everyone wanted to fight me to see if they could beat me up.
> *(David, aged 15)*

And Dermot, in Northern Ireland, had a reputation that constantly brought violence his way:

> I get hassled by the cops all the time. Even the Protestants
> round my age down round L area and B Street and all, they
> all know my name and…just because of my name they all
> want to batter me. Then if I hadn't got that name, if I was
> brought up somewhere else I wouldn't be wile into violence.
> *(Dermot, aged 15)*

Some, like Colm, acknowledged but disparaged the respect born of violence, and the way some people he observed tried to ingratiate themselves with the 'fighters':

> There's like some people in our year like, and because they're
> good fighters, everybody respects them in case they hit them
> but like what's the point? If they were bad to you I would just
> say – I wouldn't talk to them but there's people just worship
> them, people's all talk to them all the time and they just hit
> them, but the people always go back and try and make friends.
> *(Colm, aged 13)*

Elliott, aged 13, living in London, was also sceptical about the sincerity of the respect shown by people towards the 'toughies' who did the fighting. As also suggested in the chapter on bullying, respect can often be confused with fear:

> I don't think like all the toughies get respect, people are just scared of them, so they'll pretend to respect them, but really in their mind they just think they're false.
> *(Elliott)*

Young people's conflation of respect and fear is something that needs to be unravelled. Similarly, the admiration that some feel for fighting skills may not be equivalent to respect. So does fighting really produce respect for the fighters? Or just the one that wins? It is a dubious sort of respect in this day and age when physical strength is less relevant than it used to be. But respect of he (or she) who fights and wins, usually provided that they are on the side of 'right' is a philosophy supported in the media, in many films and television dramas. And it still seems to exist, especially in cultures where violence is part of normal life, such as in disadvantaged inner-city areas, or in areas of historic community conflict. There is also some evidence that young people ascribe behaviour such as fighting other pupils, and bullying, as characteristics of the popular people within a school. Fighting to achieve local respect may be one reason, but there are other reasons for getting into a fight, such as self-defence, and family honour.

Self-defence

> **Bobby:** Sometimes people call you, so you have to fight a person to show the person that you can actually batter them.
> **Andy:** If it was personal and they were calling you – got to respect yourself haven't you. They might come up to you and start beating you to death, so you've got to fight back.
> *(13–14-year-olds)*

> If you don't hit them back they're just going to keep coming and doing it again.
> *(Trevor, aged 13)*

Although there was quite a lot of feeling that violence and respect do not go together, there was strong evidence of a grudging respect for people who would defend themselves, and this implied they would fight back in some situations. This brought in things like name-calling and other bullying tactics, to which young people thought it appropriate to respond with a fight, especially in the areas characterised by violence, like Northern Ireland. This was the home of Corinne, Orla, and Ella:

> If you can fight you would have respect, so you would, nobody would say nothing to you, they just look up to you. They'd say 'I wouldn't say nothing bad about her 'cos she'll kill you', or something like that…Respect. If you can fight – if you can stick up for yourself, now say someone's shout at you, call you names or whatever, and you stick up for yourself, you'll get respect or whatever, for standing up for yourself.
> *(Corinne, aged 16)*

> If you stand up for yourself then you are respected because then others will say – they know you're going to stand up for yourself.
> *(Orla, aged 15)*

And Ella, from the same school commented:

> If you respect yourself, everybody else will too.

It was the perceived reasons for fighting that served to morally justify whether fighting was appropriate or not. Self-defence, and standing up for yourself involve taking much the same stance, and recur in many discussions of bullying as well as fighting. The advocating of 'standing up for yourself' in a bullying situation was discussed in more detail in the chapter on bullying. It was these that were seen as the most justifiable reasons for the use of violence for both sexes. In certain situations, and locations, young women felt required to stand up for themselves as much as their male peers, as Tanya, aged 14, from a disadvantaged inner-city area in the North of England, described:

> …about a couple of months ago, two girls from this school
> come starting with me and it was only me on my own but I
> got 'em back, both of 'em back, things like that,…if you
> don't stick up for yourself, I'd be getting called every day
> won't I? So you might as well stick up for yourself.
> *(Tanya)*

For some young people, sorting things out with a fight, hitting someone back, was seen as a faster and more efficient way of sorting a situation out than trying to talk, as some also felt about parental discipline (Chapter 2.) For Tanya (quoted above), the option of talking as a response was inadequate, as you would be perceived to be scared:

> No-one bullies me now, don't even say nothing to me. Not
> people from this school, like this girl out of school, she used
> to bully me and one day she hit me and I got dead mad so I
> had her a fight – and then we're talking now, that's all she
> wanted me to do is fight her. Yeah I think it does [sort things
> out], not talking, 'cause if you talk, they just think, well she's
> scared of me.
> *(Tanya)*

In some more violent areas, there was an assumption of the risk of an unprovoked attack. The need to defend oneself in this situation was described on several occasions, such as by this group of 12- to 13-year-olds, who advocated verbal negotiation but violent retaliation was the bottom line:

> **Paul:** But say someone comes up to you and hits you, like
> you're bound to hit back, aren't you.
> **Guy:** You've got to stand up for yourself…you're not going
> to want to get your face smashed in, are you?
> **Mat:** You'd try and sort it out first though, wouldn't you? To
> see if it'll stop.
> **Guy:** You could talk to them but then if they carry on hitting
> you and then you'll have to use violence, won't you?
> **Mat:** You could walk away from them.

There were some voices recommending a non-violent response to attacks, such as Mat (above), but his suggestion of simply walking away would be denounced as totally ineffective by some, such as Lauren's sister who, a fighter herself, constantly encouraged Lauren to fight and stick up for herself, but she was not persuaded:

> Like I'll try and get her out of the fights and she'll try and
> get me in 'em you know, to stick up for meself, but I don't, I
> always worm me way out of it 'cos I just don't like fighting
> 'cos I don't see the point of it.
> *(Lauren, aged 14)*

Audrey, in Northern Ireland, pointed out how hitting someone back can escalate things so that it eventually becomes a whole group of people fighting:

> Sometimes people won't listen like, but if you hit them it's
> like only making things worse and then it brings more
> people into it…then everybody comes round to see and then
> everybody else starts arguing and then they all start – piling
> in, so it's like two groups fighting.

While the young people themselves generally saw it as morally good to 'stand up for yourself', this was also the advice given by some parents, whose views on this may encourage or condone this kind of violence:

> My mum says if someone hits you, you hit them back…My
> mum says even if they're bigger than you or if they hit you
> and you pick up something, you make sure they – when you
> hit them, they go down and stay down.
> *(Kelly, aged 12)*

Self-defence is the acceptable moral stand for violence. From a peaceful distance, it is easy to advocate discussion or other non-physical ways of dealing with conflict situations, but for some young people in certain places and situations it is not seen as an effective option. It is the more violent cultures that also tend to be in the more disadvantaged working-class areas, where the expression of masculinity in particular still tends to involve using physical rather than verbal means (Laberge and Albert 1999, Katz and Buchanan 1999). Responding physically with a fight can appear to be a short, sharp way of settling things.

Fighting to defend the family or others

> I know what's right when, like, there's somebody calling me
> family something, I'm going to have a fight with them.
> *(Tanya, aged 14)*

Defending or avenging the family for some physical or verbal injury was seen as a special moral case for fighting. Where the honour or integrity of the family or one of its members had been insulted, a defence or attack had to be made if at all possible, and it often appeared more attractive and satisfying to use physical rather than verbal means. In the sectarian conflict in Northern Ireland, acts of verbal or physical abuse against members of a family from the opposing religion could provoke strong retaliation, as described in Chapter 5, but in the English locations too, 'cussing' and slurs against people often provoked a quick defence of family members, or family honour.

Discussion about fighting brought up the question of those who were seen as 'good' at fighting and their related fighting activities. Some of them seemed to use their talents in a more community-spirited way, and would stick up for other people who they saw being bullied, like Matthew:

> I always try and stick up for them, but that would have got
> me in most fights…it would be me myself (sorting out) like
> you know if I seen somebody getting, you know, slagged in
> school, I wouldn't, I don't like that happening you know.
> *(Matthew, aged 13)*

Another was Dermot, in Northern Ireland, who has a reputation for his fighting achievements, so people don't want to tackle him. He had taken it upon himself to 'defend' an old woman who lived locally and had been verbally abused as she walked to her home. In their own discussion he learned that this was not her first experience of bullying, and it is perhaps those like her who have grown up with bullying who almost seem to attract just the sort of behaviour from others that they feel fearful and vulnerable about:

> I help an old woman who lives up in ——. People would call
> her names, wee woman and all. I walked her up the road a
> couple of times so nobody would call her names…'Cos when
> I'm old and everybody else's old, they wouldn't like people

running after them'uns calling them'uns names. She was
telling me that when she was younger she got bullied about
the house and that, and she's still getting bullied even
though she's that age. It just ain't right.
(Dermot, aged 15)

It is not just young men who are fighting and defending more vulnerable
people. For example, Luu, originally from Vietnam, was brought up London,
and was the eldest of her sisters and brothers. As the eldest, aged 14 at this time,
she had had to take a fighting role in defending her young sister from being
bullied at the Chinese school they both attended. She was very clear on what
she was fighting for and about, and her mother had made it clear that fighting
must only be done for good reason, and she should not be the one to start a
fight. Thus there were strict moral guidelines within the family about the use of
violence. She describes in detail when and why she gets into fights:

It's mostly fighting I get told off for, but not in this school,
'cos you can get excluded or expelled. I have sort of got a
reputation because my cousins, we're sort of like in a family
of fighting you see, sort of like tradition...I only fight for
special reasons. Like something to defend my family, to try
and defend my family. I wouldn't fight first, I would try and
sort it out by talking to that person, ask them to stop it but if
they start, well I have to take that thing, try an' calm down,
be normal, and then if they're really out of order, I think I
have to start and then the teacher will get my parents in –
but my mum knows what I fight for, 'cos she knows, she told
me before, that if I fight, fight for a good reason, and she
goes, if you are fighting, never start first, and my mum
knows that I can keep control that's why I'm not really in big
trouble most of the time.
(Luu)

She felt strongly that there was not enough awareness by teachers of the real
reasons and context for fighting. Young people got punished for fighting and if
it was, as in her case, to defend weaker members of their own family, she felt
that this was a justifiable reason and should be taken into account:

Like when we swear, [teachers] say it's wrong to do that, and when we do good work, they say keep it up and all that, and when we fight, tell us it's not good, but sometimes, they don't know why we fight, that's the problem. That's why we get in big trouble. I don't think they understand. That's why I always ask them questions like 'If he cuss your mum, what will you do then Sir?' and some teachers just sort of give me a black look. I always do that, especially at Chinese school, 'cos there's this bully who always bully my sister. I told him to stop it before I give him some difficulties, and then he didn't, so I just be aggressive and I just beat him up, and then the teacher told me off.

(Luu)

If someone close has been insulted or physically hurt, an instant reaction is often to hit back or seek the protagonists and punish them. Roger, aged 16, living in a well-off area of the Home Counties, described an incident when his brother was attacked after which he wanted to take some violent responsive action. Both he and his father had considered taking revenge for the attack, as they knew who the perpetrators were, but eventually decided against it:

If (violence) is really personal then violence can be accepted I think if it gets very personal, but especially to do with your family or your close friends…My brother was attacked on a train last year, he was badly beaten up. He knew who it was, it was 'them people' who stand outside the school gates, some of them have been expelled from the school. They just hang about looking for fights and causing trouble…they live on the council estate. He was a mess – stitches – when I saw him I was so angry I just wanted to kill them, but revenge does not solve anything does it? My friends stopped me, they said it's not worth getting into trouble over 'them people', they're not worth it…we took them to court anyway, well the police did. At the beginning me and my dad wanted to go and get them…like I said I thought about revenge but my friends talked me out of it. Just thought there is no point in getting in trouble over them sort of people. They would know who you are as well.

(Roger)

Roger lived in a relatively non-violent, middle class area of England, and his eventual course of action was through the police and the courts, a process that would have seemed totally alien to most of the Respect young people living in Northern Ireland, or those in the disadvantaged estate in the North of England. In Roger's case it was the influence of his friends that changed the outcome, and it is friends, and others, who can be effective in cooling or fanning a potentially violent situation.

Role of others

> There used to be a few fights, but there's no fights here anymore…all the friends, they sort of calm you down anyway 'cos friends don't – people used to want to see fights a lot more but people don't really want to see that many fights anymore, so they're sort of holding back their friends, like if their friend is going to get in a fight, they'll say, 'Oh, no, calm down, talk about it.'
>
> *(Francis, aged 16)*

The expectations and behaviour of friends have an impact. Where there is a potential fight situation friends can calm you down, fire you up, or leap into the fray themselves. In certain kinds of locations, for example, the middle-class rural area in the study where Francis (quoted above) lived, where there was no real culture of fighting, friends seemed to be more often expected to have a calming influence and prevent a potential fight.

Greg's friend had also calmed him down, but his situation was a bit different. He lived in a disadvantaged area in the North of England where violence was a fact of life. He would still be joining in with it too, if it had not been for his best friend:

> If anyone called me I just used to jump into a fight straight away, but now, now I learned from him not to fight…me friend like calmed me down and said – if I got called he'd say 'Ignore it, just ignore it, it'll be OK right'. I just learned from him not to just fight back. Fighting back mentally. Like they keep calling me, they're going to get bored of it and go away. And it did do that…his Mum just taught him not to do it, and he told me 'Don't. Just ignore them.'
>
> *(Greg, aged 14)*

But in such locations where fighting was the norm, it was more often the case that friends were expected to support each other by more active means. The assumption was made that they would fight for their friends, and they similarly expected their friends to fight for or with them if necessary, as Glen commented:

> I would fight – if your girlfriend was punched or something,
> or if friends were in trouble, I would fight for my friends.
> I would hope my friends would fight for me.
> *(Glen, aged 15)*

Tanya, aged 14, who, like Glen, lived on a working-class estate in the North of England, had a group of close female friends and one characteristic of their friendship was that they could depend on one another for verbal and physical defence:

> **Tanya:** I've know them for years, they're like me sisters or
> something. We stick up for each other, we stick together in
> everything, we do everything together.
> **Interviewer:** And you say they're not a good influence on
> you, in what sort of way?
> **Tanya:** Like fighting and arguing but…I'm not bothered
> really 'cause I'd do anything for them and they know I will,
> just like they'd do anything for me.

But on the whole the role of friends in a fight situation depended partly on location. Where violence was commonplace, most thought friends should physically defend each other, where violence is rare, they stop potential participants from getting involved. In any discussion or programme to curb bullying and fighting, it is perhaps worth untangling what the most helpful role of friends could be.

Gender and fighting

Young women fighting

> **Interviewer:** What do you have to do to be hard apart from
> going round threatening people?
> **Charlotte:** You have to practically show it don't you?
> **Rosie:** Yeah, like women fighting – things like that.
> **Sharon:** You've got to win all the fights and do it on your
> own rather than with everyone there, fighting for you.
> *(13–14-year-olds)*

> Some of the wee girls beat the crap out of any wee fella, like
> a wee girl I hang around with, Leanne, she would kill any
> wee fella out of school, she would. She's a man, we call her a
> man.
> *(Aideen, aged 14)*

It is clear from the experiences of many young women already quoted, that
fighting is a common feature of their lives, if not as much as the young men.
Fighting is not just a male preserve, and there are young women, such as
Leanne (referred to above) who can clearly hold their own when it comes to
physical violence. There is, however, a lack of British literature on girls and
violence as most research has been on boys and young men. There have been
some studies, such as Anne Campbell's research on girls and delinquency in the
late 1970s and early 1980s (Campbell 1989), and a more recent study by
Burman, Brown and Batchelor (2003), which looked at the meaning of violence
and violent behaviour from the viewpoint of girls.

Campbell explored the nature and incidence of girls and fighting. Her sample
was girls from working-class areas in England and Scotland. Most of them had
seen a fight and almost nine out of ten had been involved in one. She noted
that more girls who were going around in a mixed group of boys and girls got
involved in fights, rather than those in all-girl groups. Yet almost three-quarters
of all the fights described happened between girls, either in the street or at
school. Most were with their friends when these occurred. Their fights were
mainly with one other girl, but in half the cases, their friends came to help
them out. Although over half disagreed that fighting was only for boys, the

general attitude to fighting was negative. Although to some extent they expressed moral disapproval of fighting, they contradicted this when discussing a concrete situation of reacting to someone backing out of a fight, when they were condemnatory, seeing such behaviour as 'chicken'. Campbell found no indication that the girls felt they were contravening their 'femininity' by fighting, and on the contrary, in some situations the boys were encouraging them to fight. But fighting in the case of girls, was seen as something to be eventually cast off with maturity and an adult status.

Michele Burman and others (Burman, Brown and Batchelor 2003) focused on 13- to 16-year-old-girls from various backgrounds and areas in Scotland. They found that although the girls did not use the term much themselves, 'violence' was interpreted widely to describe and categorise a range of incidents, both physical and non-physical. Its interpretation also depended on the social or situational context. They recorded high levels of verbal abuse, which many considered to be even more harmful and damaging than physical violence. This was especially in the context of the importance of girls' friendships, whereby a 'falling out' can lead to verbal abuse and someone becoming the target of malicious gossip from ex-friends. The targets for verbal abuse were, like for others, often family members, especially mothers, and most girls spoke of the desirability of 'standing up' for their family and friends. The vast majority described violence as a 'bad' thing, but also recognised their own potential for using it. However, the Burman study showed that only a minority of these girls got involved with fighting (about 5 per cent). When such violence does happen, it meaningfully 'serves to maintain group solidarity, reinforces friendships, affirms allegiances and enhances personal status'. But this is not to deny that some girls find physical violence abhorrent and others are extremely ambivalent about it. Burman, Brown and Batchelor concluded that their research has shown 'how the meaning of violence for girls, is at once complex, contradictory, contingent and constantly shifting, and bound up with their situations, experiences, identities and relationships'.

In the cultures of violence we have described, many of the Respect young women were no strangers to violence. One familiar aspect that emerged was the gendered nature of fighting – that girls fight in different ways from boys, as the quotes below illustrate:

> Aye, pulling hair an' all. Wee girls are wile bitchy. They
> scrape with nails an' all, even in class.
> *(Emma, aged 15)*

> **Orla:** I mean boys fight all the time when they're carrying on. Wee girls wouldn't scrap.
> **Ella:** No, but wee girls would threaten. They'd say – 'I'll get you'.
> *(15–16-year-olds)*

These kinds of descriptions are not new, and such female fighting techniques have been portrayed on film and TV, as well as being played out by participants on the Jerry Springer Show. With the movement towards women being more involved in physical contact sports such as women's football, and martial arts, it might be thought that female techniques of fighting might have changed, but seemingly not.

The emotional style of fighting was also seen to be gendered. Girls would take fights more personally and as a consequence, wouldn't speak to each other for a long time afterwards. Boys on the other hand, were considered to have a fight and it's over and done with and they are friends again:

> Everyone says girls' fights are always worse 'cos of what they do. Boys don't really take it to heart or anything, but girls, girls – girls are softer…and arguments go on for days and days until they fall out – have arguments for days. They're more sensitive.
> *(Carla, aged 14)*

> Boys, like with boys, they have arguments and fights but they're more, they can – with boys they can have an argument and the next day they're friends, but they can have a fight and the next week like they're all running around playing football together, all friends and everything but with girls it's different, when they have a fight or argument they stay away from each other for a long, long time.
> *(Shirleen, aged 13)*

This may be related to young women's propensity to use verbal rather than physical aggression, or to adopt social exclusion as a bullying tactic, or simply the rearrangement of friendship patterns that seems to be very much a characteristic of girls' culture. In the Respect study, young women expressed a high level of concern about changing friendships, especially during the younger years, which was absent for young men.

One view of femininity disapproves of fighting by girls and women. Females are considered by some to be the weaker sex and are expected to behave accordingly. In this role they would then be respected by boys and men. However, equality does not mean being as physically aggressive as boys. Women do not get respect from fighting, unless they are absolutely brilliant, as depicted by some movies such as *Lara Croft: Tomb Raider, Crouching Tiger, Hidden Dragon,* and *Red Sonja.* But girls can and do fight, usually with other girls, and female fighting is nothing unusual in areas characterised by violence and disadvantage. In these areas it fits with the general pattern of violence experienced by both sexes within the home, at school and on the streets.

Boys hitting girls

> I don't know why – they're not scared to hit girls. They would hit girls without thinking twice about it, which I think then they probably see at home. I don't think it's right that boys should hit girls ever.
> **(Shannon, aged 13)**

In Chapter 2, a gender contradiction was described in that boys were not meant to hit girls, and were often taught this at home and at school, and yet it was clear that domestic violence usually involved a man hitting a woman. Therefore the logic appeared to be that at a certain age, it was not uncommon, although not generally acceptable, for males to hit females. This came up again when fighting was discussed. The general feeling was that boys and young men should not hit girls, as Shannon (above) endorsed. And yet in more violent cultures, it seemed fairly commonplace, as 14-year-old Charlotte, from Northern England, described:

> …a lot of lads would love to punch girls but won't – but there's a lot of lads that do it now though, isn't there? A lot of lads do it for the fun of it – for the joke. But it can hurt. I mean they like give you bruises and dead legs.
> **(Charlotte)**

In Campbell's research the girls spoke of being hit by boys who were not boyfriends, and although they did not like it, the consensus was that if they could hit boys then they should be willing to accept the converse (Campbell

1989). For some 12- to 13-year-old boys in London, if seemed very unfair that girls were able to give them a whack but they were not meant to hit back:

> **Trevor:** ...sometimes it's out of order because your mum says don't hit girls, yeah? But one day they might just come up to you and start pulling your hair and beating you up on the floor and you can't do nothing.
> **Pelu:** It was worse in primary school – every time a girl would come up to me and start trouble for no reason – if I slapped a girl now my mum, who taught me to hit back, would come telling me again 'Why did you do that? Who told you to hit them?' And she's telling me that.

This group discussed this disparity further, pointing out how boys and young men in their position were in a no-win situation with regard to hitting girls back, because if you didn't do so, they might walk all over you or call you a 'poofter', and if you did, you were in danger of being called a sissy for hitting those who were (theoretically) weaker than you:

> **Kelly:** If a boy hits a girl I think that boy's got to regret his life then...
> **Trevor:** That's unfair though, that's a liberty 'cos if like ten girls come up to one boy, right, and started beating him up, well he can't do nothing and if he won, he'd be called – because his mum probably told him, right, not to hit a girl, right?
> **Harry:** If he runs he's going to be a poofter, if he hits them he's going to be a sissy.
> **Trevor:** He's just stuck.

Being a fighter

> It's a fighting area round here...there's always fights up round here...never go anywhere without seeing fights and all that...It's just like loads of big rumbles and – see, there's a bottom area, a middle area, and a top area, and you get all of them having big rucks and fights...I'm in the middle...I have fights with anyone!
> *(David, aged 15)*

> It ain't that I'm good at fighting, it's just that I don't give up
> – you can't really say you're good at fighting because there's
> always someone that's better than you…some people stop
> after someone goes on the floor, but I don't. I'd always keep
> on doing it until someone has to pull me off.
> *(Kerby, aged 16)*

In some ways, fighting was seen as a skill or an art and those who were good at it tended to use it to gain a name for themselves, at least up to a certain age. If you were weak, or no good at fighting, it makes no sense to be getting in fights all the time. So logically, many of those who do get into a lot of fights, are people with more strength or skill than others. Then they get a reputation for it (as David did in Northern Ireland) and others look to beat them, much like the gunfighters featured in Western movies. Once a person has a reputation for something like fighting, it is hard to either get rid of it, or stop others from acting provocatively or violently in order to see how good that reputation was. It can prove an individual cycle that is hard to stop. In David's case, it was also linked to his family's reputation, and in violent cultures, it is not difficult for a whole family to become identified as a 'fighting family'.

Among a number of young men in the Respect study whose lives were characterised by some kind of violence, 15-year-old Kofi, and 16-year-old Kerby, were both young men living in London who had been at the same school (though in different years). They talked more specifically about their experiences as people who had constantly found themselves in fights. Bearing in mind the difficulty of shedding such a reputation, they each claimed to have changed their attitudes over recent years, mainly because of the influence of one of their parents, their father and mother respectively. Kofi's father had himself been in prison for beating up a man who tried to rob him in the street, and Kofi had been suspended from school many times for fighting. This would have had grave consequences for his education, but his father's influence was helping him to walk away from situations, instead of getting into them. Asked whether he still did a lot of fighting, Kofi replied:

> Naw, not now. This was just then. People used to get on my
> nerves and I had a short temper, so as soon as people got on
> my nerves…But I sorted myself out I just decided, well this
> ain't doing anything, doing me no favours and to do
> well…I…school and being suspended every five minutes

ain't getting me into work. Stay here, just sorted it out. Just
ignore people if they started getting on my nerves – and I
noticed it worked. My dad was a bit angry that I kept getting
suspended. He just said like it's not the right way to go about
it, just ignore them, don't start getting in any mess.
(Kofi)

Kofi was managing to control his aggressive responses and was still getting
through school. Kerby also had a history of fighting, which had always got him
into trouble. It seemed too, that he had been able to inflict quite a lot of harm
on those who he got involved with, some of whom had ended up in hospital.
But he had a lot of respect for his mother, who could remonstrate with him and
would still give him a slap although he was now much bigger than her. He had
grown up with a certain amount of physical violence, which he saw as quite
normal, as he commented: 'my cousins beat me anyway, all my friends when
they beat me, they used to hold me down and beat me'. Violence produces
more violence, and this is a hard circle to break. He was very quick to anger,
which he found hard to control on numerous occasions, such as if people did
not pay him money they owed, or someone insulted him or his mother. His
mother had an influence over him and he claimed that she had persuaded him
that talking was a better option, and he was beginning to be more in control of
his feelings:

> I've got more calm and peace with (my mum) because she
> sat down and talked to me more. Because when I was
> younger I was like if something happened to me I'd come in
> and get a knife or something and go back out, gonna do
> them or something, but now, I'd rather talk it out than use
> violence now, because my mum sat down and talked to me,
> saying yeah, that's getting you into trouble – because that's
> got me in a lot of trouble before – where there's been loads
> of people looking for me and I can't go into that area
> because there's too much people looking for me, so I just
> talk it out now. I still got a temper that I can't control but
> I'm, I'm starting to control it more.

Despite his mother's reasoning with him, his claims to be talking instead of
fighting, and the high hopes he expressed of himself and his best friend setting
up a business together, his future could be jeopardised by his continuing

propensity for violence. Kerby contradicted a lot of his own declarations of change. He had left school but he had not left his fighting days behind. In fact, he observed how since leaving and not being in school uniform, he had had even more fights. As long as he perceived a 'need' for fighting in any situation, there was a risk of escalating violence which could one day get Kerby into real trouble:

> Fighting – it is gonna get me into trouble. I know when it's needed and when it's not needed – like I was in the pub the other day, and I beat up, well lately I've beat up two boys badly and I've put two boys in hospital and the other day I beat up some boy, broke his nose…but, I don't make no trouble, I just make friends, I just wanna go out and make friends, but if there's trouble to me, I confront it.

Kofi and Kerby came from a background where fighting was quite common, if not condoned. By contrast, some 16-year-old young men growing up in a leafy middle-class area of the Home Counties did not share these sorts of experiences and saw little need, at their age, for any kind of physical skirmish:

> **Francis:** There used to be a few fights but there's no fights here anymore.
> **Roger:** It's just in the school at parties, someone does something, you occasionally get pushed up against a wall but you rarely get punches or anything.
> **Edward:** Because people no longer feel as much that they have to fight to prove something.
> **Roger:** A lot of the time you don't need to fight, say someone was abusing you and you went up and spoke to them and warned them…once they know that you're not going to put up with it they might think, better stop now or I'll get into trouble.
> **Edward:** If you've got self-respect and you just stand up to someone and don't give up, people don't push it so much.
> **Roger:** If there's any fighting there's a couple of scuffles maybe at parties and stuff, but a lot of that's to do with alcohol.

But although numerous studies have identified working-class masculinities typified by toughness and violence (for example, Willis 1977, Mac An Ghail 1994, Cohen 1997, Laberge and Albert 1999), it must be kept in mind that young people are not passively inscribed within social class or gendered prescriptions, and do have agency to produce their own identities. These may, of course, be in keeping with, for instance the violent (or non-violent) nature of their environment.

To some extent, there was a culture and narrative of 'fighting talk' involving past incidents and future intentions, both of which may be subject to exaggeration. Present talking and future reality can be quite different, but such narratives can represent a moral communication as well as self expression. Fighting is often depicted in the media as a kind of art form or admired skill, and in films and on TV the best fighter is often the hero who destroys his (or her) enemies and wins the day. But fighting in everyday life is not so glamourous or advantageous. It may solve an immediate situation for the winner(s), but often leads to more violence, as well as exclusion from school or college, and even trouble with the law. They often discover that violence is a high risk strategy that can escalate out of control. It can undermine the process of becoming an autonomous moral subject. The young people may not see fighting as the 'right' action to take, but the underlying moral justifications and imperatives involved need to be considered and understood.

Key points

1. Fighting is seen as legitimate and necessary in disadvantaged urban areas characterised by cultures of violence such as those involved in this research in northern England and Northern Ireland.
2. In a similar way to the situation of bullying, fighting and being a good fighter was seen as a way of gaining some kind of respect, once more confounded by fear (as also described in Thomson and others 2001).
3. The main reasons legitimising fighting were in self-defence and in defence of another person or the family honour. Once more, 'standing up for yourself' was an important concept in this.
4. The role of friends as pacifiers or as escalators of a violent situation can be important. In cultures of non-violence it was the former, and the latter in more violent environments.

5. There are certain gender issues and differences – girls fight as well as boys, although less so and in different ways, and there is a contradiction for young men about (not) fighting or hitting girls.

6. Fighting was more common among younger age groups and decreased with time, but less so in areas characterised by adult violence.

7. The meaning and significance of fighting in any situation has to be considered. In some situations and cultures, talking things through is not seen as an option by young people, even if they disapprove of violence in general.

5 Violence in the community

> It's tradition as well, about that sort of thing, isn't it? People
> hold different views, like, different cultures where violence is
> the key.
> *(Francis, aged 16)*

There are cultures where violence is the key, as Francis observed. In the Respect
project, there were two locations that were clearly characterised by cultures of
violence. These were in Northern Ireland, and in the North of England, and
both were characterised by relative poverty and the run-down nature of much of
the local urban environment. The location in London also had some incidence
of violence within the general community, but it was not such a violent local
culture. The other locations represented more cultures of non-violence: both
were in the countryside, one around a rural village area, and the other in a leafy
middle-class Home Counties area. This chapter explores the two main cultures
of violence in the project, but not in equal proportions. There was a wealth of
material from the four Northern Ireland schools describing the views and
experiences of the young people there, who were in a particularly extreme
situation of conflict in the late 1990s, and proportionally less from the North of
England, and this is reflected in this chapter, which explores the legacy and the
legitimacy of the continuing violence in these areas for these young people.

Sectarian violence in Northern Ireland

> They just want to know if you're a Protestant or a Catholic.
> And if you're in the wrong area, like, that's you hammered,
> you might as well book your hospital place now...It's stupid
> like, 'cos like we have to live in the same country, we might

as well get along instead of all this fighting and, there
already has been 25 years of tit for tat killing you know like –
'we'll kill a Protestant' and 'we'll kill yours'.
(Neville, aged 16)

At the end of the day it's us that have to live with it. I don't
think it's right, older people going out and fighting and all
for what they believe in and then leaving it all to other
people to pick up the pieces, and if they kill somebody it's
not them that has to suffer...
(Bronwyn, aged 14)

The Respect data was collected at the same time as there were significant
developments and crises in the 'peace process' in Northern Ireland. These
young people's views were being collected in the context of paramilitary
ceasefires and their collapse, political talks, sectarian murder atrocities, the
Good Friday Agreement, and the establishment of new political government
bodies. Although there seemed to be a lot of changes occurring which for some
signalled a new hope and optimism for the future of Northern Ireland, for
others it intensified their distrust and uncertainty. While new talks of peace
made headlines in the news, there was still violence going on at street level.

The conflict in Northern Ireland has claimed more than 3,500 lives since 1969,
which represent about one in 500 people within a population of 1.5 million. As
well as the deaths, many thousands have been seriously injured, and research
suggests that almost half of all adults have personally known someone killed as a
result of political violence. Residential segregation, based on the two main
religious communities, Catholic and Protestant, has continued to be a feature of
life in Northern Ireland since the beginning of what has come to be known as
'the Troubles'. This segregation means that about half the population live in
areas exclusively populated by their own religion. The effect of this is to create a
threatening situation for those, for example, who live on the edges of two
opposing communities, and those who for some reason cross over the
boundaries either geographically, or through the development of cross-religious
relationships.

Northern Ireland is a young community in which over 40 per cent are under
the age of 24 (NISRA). The children and young people grow up in the
knowledge of the segregation and religious antagonism that exists around them.
They may find some overlap in various mixed religion schools, but their social

and leisure space tends to follow divided lines. The young people from Northern Ireland in the Respect study often referred to a concept of 'purity'. A 'pure' area was one that was traditionally totally Catholic or Protestant, and which defined itself by being separate and different, tried to keep its border up and resisted or repelled outsiders (McGrellis 2002). The young people defined their own and other areas in terms of their relative 'purity' of being completely one religion or the other. Such 'pure' spaces foster and fuel common identities, and prevent the intermingling of different identities. The people who tend to guard the sectarian nature of these communities are young people, and more specifically the young men, who have clearly been the ones most affected and suffering from the Troubles. McGrellis (2002) has written about the relationship of this purity and the resulting bitterness that it fosters in the people living within these areas. Tension is fuelled in these areas of high insecurity, where much effort is spent trying to protect against outsiders and maintain social control and cohesion. The result is often the violent acts that have characterised the Troubles and contributed to the bitterness that permeates these communities.

> I think it's the people that are so bitter that they can't get past a person's religion or whatever they are. Me myself, I don't have time for the IRA or the UVF – I don't care for what they do, either of them like. It doesn't matter.
> *(Tina, aged 16)*

Fuelling the conflict

> The big religion thing – it's just killing everybody just because of their religion or what they do or what they are. I mean it's not right. I think it's very childish going after people.
> *(Shannon, aged 13)*

The Northern Irish young people in the Respect study were well acquainted with the violence that has characterised their country for many years. Some of them and their families had had painful experiences of the sectarian violence. For them violence was to some extent part of their local culture, a way of life, whether or not they agreed with any of it, and many of them did not. Many, for example, described the continuing violence between the two communities as stupid or childish, and were very much against it. Some, like Shannon (quoted above) and Adele thought that it was originally a religious conflict that had created its own historical momentum but now was being perpetuated by people without a lot of sense or maturity, or education:

> I think people forget what it's about. It's meant to be about
> tradition and all that there. It's just a cause to fight about
> now...At the end of the day it's like – it started off as a
> Christian belief and now it's just these ones that haven't got
> an ounce of sense. I think most of the terrorists must really
> like dozzos, didn't do well at school. If they think it's OK to
> go out and shoot some 19-year-old because he's a Catholic,
> they need a kick up the...
> *(Adele, aged 16))*

They endorsed that few people liked political violence, and no one enjoys it. Several, like Orla, commented on how as a religious conflict, it often seemed to have little religious commitment attached to it, but just a prolongation of fighting between sectarian groups:

> No I don't think – I think that's totally stupid, political
> violence. Aye, 'cos what's the point in fighting? It's never
> going to solve anything. When you think about it, what are
> they fighting over anyway – they're just different religions and
> half them – you have to admit, half of them don't even believe
> in their religion. Most of them don't even go to Mass.
> *(Orla, aged 16)*

According to some of the young people the antagonism between the Catholic and Protestant communities was fuelled by the media, who repeatedly reminded people that they were not meant to like one another, as Roma observed:

> We don't really understand what's the difference you know,
> nobody can understand, especially not us, especially like
> Catholic and Protestant and all that there. There's too much
> TV and it's going into your heads that all right, we're not
> meant to like Protestants, we're not meant to like Catholics.
> We are this and we're not allowed to like them. So it's the
> TV's trying to put to you – we're Catholic, we're not allowed
> to like Protestants.
> *(Roma, aged 14)*

Another reinforcement of this conflict was played out on the football field, as the different communities supported the respective football teams in Scotland – Celtic (Catholic) and Rangers (Protestant) – and young men could not go into certain areas wearing the colours of their team without risking a violent attack from the supporters of the other team:

> **Jimmy:** There's plenty of people that – different Rangers' things and stuff – like him there.
> **Malcolm:** You can't go over the town like, the Catholics going there with like Celtic stuff and that. If we go into town wearing Rangers' stuff you get beaten.
> **Jimmy:** You're the same way as them ones.
> **Malcolm:** Aye, I play football with them.
> *(13–14-year-olds)*

The sectarian violence was also represented and fuelled in a way by the jokes that went around between the young people. In the Respect questionnaire, the young people had been asked to give a joke or funny story that was current for them. Jokes about violence only accounted for 5 per cent of the total, but these varied by the different groups. They were more likely to be told by the older year groups, by young men, and by the young people living in Northern Ireland. In fact, nearly three-quarters of the jokes on violence came from those at the four schools in Northern Ireland. Some of these jokes were sectarian. This is an example from a 13–14-year-old young woman:

> **Q:** What's the difference between Liverpool FC and the IRA?
> **A:** Liverpool says you will never walk alone. The IRA says you will never walk again.

Bitter feelings

It was hard for young people to separate from this violence, especially when it may have involved a member of their own family, and this had fuelled the bitterness about the fighting and the 'enemy' that had permeated many families and was passed down from parents to children. Nevertheless, the Respect young people here were trying to grapple with this so that it may not become such a problem for them, and to avoid developing a bitter attitude even when a family member had been attacked, or petrol bombed or killed. Corinne, aged 16, described how her grandmother's house had been petrol bombed, seemingly without reason, and how she was trying not to react with the hate and bitterness that the Troubles have generated:

> I don't know why, I didn't hate all of them, I just hated the ones I thought it was...it was too close to home, that kind of thing. I never expected it to happen because I talk too much to Protestants and Catholics, and I get on wile well with them, and my granny and granda do...I didn't get wile bitter, I was just in shock I think. It's just them one's done it, they're just stupid and insensitive and don't care about anybody. And they just believe in what they were brought up as, nobody taught them, they were just brought up to hate Catholics no matter what age they were.
> *(Corinne)*

Corinne blamed the upbringing of those who were out committing the violence, and in a focus group discussion Carol and Donovan questioned the type of family that such violent young people came from:

> **Carol:** It's like wains that are out rioting and like where are their parents when they're throwing petrol bombs and burning out shops and things? Like what type of family do they come from if you're allowed to go out and do that?
> **Donovan:** You'd only come from a bitter background doing that, if you were allowed to do that.
> **Carol:** It's not just rioting.
> **Donovan:** It's bitterness.
> *(16-year-olds)*

As well as any political peace process, hope for peace is to some extent contained in the attitudes of up and coming generations. For many of the Respect young people living in this city in Northern Ireland, a serious concern was that they did not want their own children to grow up in the atmosphere of violence in which they had been growing up. In some cases they referred to violence being promulgated by parents, who imbued their own children from an early age with the hatred that they felt for the 'other' religion. Liam came from a strongly Catholic family in which his own father had been taught from a young age to fight and hate. In his turn, his father had expected his son to grow up acting the same:

> He (my father) was brought up at 16 years of age, standing
> in the streets having gun battles with the police, at 16. I
> mean, that influenced him growing up and the way he
> thought. And one of his brothers was nearly beaten to death
> by a soldier…Time I was sent out, by the father, out to the
> police, wi' bottles – to throw at them. I was only five or six. I
> knew, well I knew it was wrong but I thought it was right
> because that's what I was taught to do.
> *(Liam, aged 16)*

Ella resented the way older generations had left younger ones with all this fear
and violence:

> It's all going to come back on us. They're all dying, it's us
> that left to look round our shoulders the rest of our life.
> *(Ella, aged 16)*

But not all parents were like this, and Corinne described how, while her father
had grown up with violence inflicted on him and his family from Protestants,
and had developed the bitterness described earlier, her mother wanted things to
be different for her:

> I've been like good friends with Protestants, my best friend's
> a Protestant, and if everyone got on the way we got on, it
> would be class so it would. It's not just us, it's for the
> younger ones growing up…see my mammy said I don't want
> you ones having to grow up the way we had to grow up. My
> daddy like he grew up in a Protestant area and he got his
> windows and all put through all the time, and he's wile bitter
> like, and I don't want to be bitter like him, and he would say
> things to me 'Tch, you sitting down there with scum', and all
> that there. And this is me: 'Look daddy they're not all scum'.
> *(Corinne, aged 16)*

Some of the Respect young people both young women and young men, talked
of wanting their own children to grow up in a different and more peaceful
environment:

> 'Cos I don't want my wains growing up seeing f******
> bombs going off and not being able to go out with friends
> and that there.
> *(Liam, aged 16)*

> **Anna:** I don't want to be involved in a country with violence
> all the time, it just isn't good, you need a break from it.
> **Karen:** You don't want your kids to grow up like this either.
> **Anna:** I just don't like living in this, it's too VIOLENT.
> *(13–14-year-olds)*

But making a break from this pattern may be hard, especially with the continuation of segregated communities and the passage of bad feelings down through the generations. For instance, in group discussions on sectarianism held in schools by the National Children's Bureau (Kelly 2002), 16–17-year-olds spoke about the influence of parents in promoting negative views of the 'other' community, and in participating in local violence. To address this in any way must be done early, as a survey of three- to six-year-olds showed that these children were aware of their own religious identity and of sectarianism at this young age and the main influences were, understandably, the family, school and community. The onset of school experiences in particular marked a rapid increase in sectarian awareness (Connolly, Smith and Kelly 2002).

Gender and relationships

The young people in Kelly's research (2002) felt they had few opportunities to make cross-community contacts and could not envisage having a boy/girlfriend from the other community. For reasons of safety they preferred to live and socialise in areas with people of the same religious background. Both sexes experienced the violence but it was mainly the young men who were most involved, and from quite an early age. As 13-year-old Kiera said: 'The girls our age don't really care but most of the boys from here, they're all into giving hidings and starting and start big riots and all.' It is also the young men who become the guardians of the territory occupied by their particular religion. McGrellis (2002) describes how it is the young men from strongly Loyalist or Republican families who seem to automatically evolve as the leaders and custodians of their communities. They often find themselves somewhat constrained within this position, in that it is the role expected of them, and it is consequently hard to change this or even to move geographically out of the area. It is the young women who find it easier to cross boundaries or indeed leave an area altogether.

Where young women become very aware of or involved in conflict is where there are cross-religious relationships, whether same sex or opposite sex. Adele, from a Protestant family, thought that although there could be friendship, because of the underlying feelings you always went back to your own religion:

> I always think I can be friends with Catholics, but still too there'd be – 'Oh I hate that Fenian lot'. You'd still be wile violent towards them. It's always there, you always come back to your own.
> *(Adele, aged 16)*

Dermot was from a strongly Catholic background, and for him to be friends with Protestants would have a violent outcome:

> It would cause a fight like. If anybody found out I was going to meet a Protestant, there'd be a pile of wee boys with me like – wanting to fight with him. It would probably be the same with wee girls.
> *(Dermot, aged 15)*

Having a relationship with someone of the opposite religion may mean you had to meet or collect each other from the 'wrong' side of the tracks. Allan, a 15-year-old Protestant, would be cautious about having a girlfriend from a Catholic area:

> It's hard enough 'cos some people out of your family will be saying – 'Get her out of the family or you can leave too…'. If you're going with a Catholic too, it would be hard enough to if you had to go up and collect her from her place if she lived up on the top of a hill, it would be hard enough to go up there and collect her and come down with her without anybody giving you a hiding.
> *(Allan)*

In one of the focus groups, 16-year-old Janice and Ella talked rather wistfully about the possibility of there being more mixed relationships which could perhaps stop the fighting as people got to know each other better:

> **Janice:** Everyone would realise that they're all the same.
> **Ella:** It's just the religion that's different. And they might stop fighting.

Political and religious differences produce the violence and bitterness that circumscribes friendships and relationships for young people. Crossing those boundaries into mixed relationships can be very risky, and in some areas would not be tolerated at all (Sharpe 2001). For those harbouring bitterness and hatred, people who 'mix' relationships are seen to warrant the use of violence to break them up and preserve the boundaries.

Revenge

> Well I think it's wrong to use violence in politics but people
> – I'm not trying to say anything about any side – people are
> blaming other people in the wrong and then they're
> blaming them back for doing something else in the wrong
> and then violence then erupts through that. Then people go
> and kill other people and there's something called pay-back
> and then people, other people get killed for their religion.
> **(Joseph, aged 13)**

Revenge has had a high profile in Northern Ireland. Not at all surprisingly because in the context of sectarian conflict, any violent act committed by one group or the other will be avenged by friends or family, as 14-year-old Kieran describes:

> Just there were these boys and there were about six or seven
> and I was about ten and they were kicking the crap out of
> my wee cousin so they were, so me and my friend we went
> out and grabbed them and just – just cleaned the streets
> with them. Then they got their big brothers to us, and we
> got our big cousins to them and it started into a big feud.
> **(Kieran)**

Once begun, an act of revenge can reverberate back and forth between the parties. It takes on a momentum of its own which gives it meaning and legitimacy. Although those participating in the Respect study generally disapproved of someone taking revenge because it was perpetuating violence, there was acknowledgement that it could also provide satisfaction. When asked if he thought that revenge worked, Dermot answered: 'No, not really, but it makes you happier', and Aideen noted:

> I think it's sometimes good getting your own back on
> people. If somebody did something to you, it's good to know
> you can get them back…If somebody is threatening you and
> you get someone else to threaten them'uns, it's good, 'cos
> then they won't do it again like.
>
> *(Aideen, aged 14)*

The young people's logic was that avenging something would prevent it happening again, whereas in fact the opposite is often the case. Violence in the form of revenge had certainly reverberated through the minds and several lives of the young people from Northern Ireland. Discussions of this issue in the focus groups were frequent in the Northern Ireland schools, where tit-for-tat violence was very much the norm, either between families or between the political and religious communities, and often accepted as inevitable, as 16-year-old Liam described:

> There's no need for (political violence) but sometimes too,
> both sides are left with no choice, sure, look at the G area
> shooting. After that there like you couldn't expect people to
> sit back and watch that there. You knew there was going to
> be retaliation like, for it. I know a retaliation is not right but
> you knew it was going to f****** come like…Revenge is
> justice but – if you can get revenge then that's justice done
> too. Like say someone gave me a hiding like I'd look to go
> and give them a hiding then – or even maybe kill
> them…There's a prime example, – M got a hiding the other
> night. This boy he punched the f*** out of [—] at Christmas
> time, he battered him and left him on a life support
> machine, and the boy got off the life support machine and
> came with a big crowd of boys…and kicked the shite out of
> him…it just keeps going and going…now he will look for
> revenge, he'll probably try and get his younger brother if he
> can't get him…
>
> That's the way things are and it's like that and you have to live
> with it like. I don't agree with going out and shooting someone
> like. But I know if some bastard shot one of my family, I'd go
> and do it twice as hard. I'd go out and shoot two.

In Northern Ireland, the young people, particularly the young men, appeared to have little confidence in or respect for the police, many of whom were from the Protestant community. It was felt that 'justice' could not be left to them, and thus the obvious step was to take the law into your own hands. This seemed to legitimise revenge and make it more logical and effective to take the law into their own hands, as Danny and Liam asserted:

> See if you were jumped some night and you got a kicking
> and the cops wouldn't do nothing about it…it's happened to
> me before. I'd go out and look for them, get a few boys,
> carloads like, go out and get them…'cos they'll know not to
> then, they'll know better.
> *(Danny, aged 15)*

> You go down the town some night and you get a kicking, you
> get a hiding, you go to the police and report the hiding right,
> and instead of taking the law into your own hands you say,
> right, I'll do the right thing, and you go to the police to
> report it. They sort of more or less turn their nose up at you
> and say 'Go away, we can't deal with that there', and then so
> you say, well, oh f***, I went to the law and they decided
> they're not going to do anything with it so I will take the law
> into my own hands now, sometimes you're left with no choice.
> *(Liam, aged 16)*

But despite the apparent logic supporting the need for revenge or pay-back, there were many voices speaking against such tit-for-tat actions. Margaret for example, advocated talking together:

> [Revenge] shouldn't happen. If somebody killed they should
> sit down and say why – because suppose they were doing
> stuff against them, they don't have to kill them, they just
> have to sit down together and talk to them.
> *(Margaret, aged 12)*

But this would be hard in the context of the historical background and the high levels of feeling that were likely to be running amongst the people involved in any long-standing feud. Perhaps at the age of 12 it seems relatively straightforward to suggest talk instead of fight, but by the time many young people reach the age of 15 or 16 (which many of those quoted here had done), their increased knowledge and experience of the situation have made them more aware of the complexities involved.

Michelle, aged 14, who went to school in an exclusively Protestant area, blamed the segregation of the communities for contributing to the violence and bitterness that seemed to go on and on and she advocated more mixing of the two sides:

> I think if you are actually kept apart people get more bitter because if they seen somebody going past they would be determined to get them, you know? But if you're in amongst them sometimes you know, it wouldn't be too bad because you would be used to them. But if you're kept apart for a long time it will get really bad.
> *(Michelle)*

The streets where these young people lived were seen somewhat differently to those in most other areas of the UK. Personal safety depended on being careful about where you went, and who you were with. Going into areas that were strongly inhabited by the 'opposite' religious group could be dangerous, and socialising with them could be equally so. Over the years there had been many incidents of violence, revenge attacks and even killings, of which the young people were well aware:

> Anybody, a Catholic or Protestant, can't go into any other estate without getting harassed or getting hit or anything.
> *(Gemma, aged 14)*

Since this time when the young people in the Respect study were discussing their experiences of violence there has been some improvement in the situation through the peace talks and cease-fires. But there is not yet a real negotiated peace, and there is still a significant level of tension for them at street and school level between the communities. It has been suggested that there is a different kind and more chaotic kind of violence characterising the post-peace-talks situation (McGrellis 2003). Most people, young or old, would say they want a peaceful resolution however hard it may seem to envisage. A study by the University of Ulster (referred to by Hari 2002) suggested that under-25s were the most sectarian group in Northern Ireland. Nevertheless, it is perhaps up to the younger generations to try and pull up the deep roots of bitterness.

Well, things, things that I was, I always felt was strong in our house, that, erm, good discipline and all that, and, and Ireland should be united, and Brits should pull out the morrow, and you should do whatever it takes to get rid of them. If it means murder, well so be it. That's what I was taught when I was younger, but now I know. I've learnt that's not the way, 'cause by you going out and killing someone, it's only over a piece of land, and we've seen it and we've seen the bombings and the shootings for the last 25 years and it hasn't worked, or 300 years, and it hasn't worked in 300 years. I don't think it's going to work now. The only way, is try and get on together, whatever the country decides, whatever the majority wants, we've just got to go by it. It's not worth dying over any more. Too many graves full up, so there is, and too many people hurt, too many people lost.
(Liam, aged 16)

Community violence in England

The other area in the Respect study where there was a culture of violence and hence quite a high level of community violence was situated in the North of England. Most of the young people in this location lived and went to school in a disadvantaged working-class area where unemployment was high, housing was bad, family breakdown was frequent, there was poor health, and a paucity of facilities. This violence was not politically motivated or religion driven, it was simply born out of a culture that makes survival hard in general.

In this area, it was common to find yourself in danger from attack on the streets, which could escalate, as these 15- to 16-year-olds described:

Yvonne: You could be innocently with some friends, and another group come up and they've got – not weapons – you know…

Owen: Batons…

Yvonne: …which they use anyways – could use these – try and use these and then say one falls. To get out of that situation you'd probably pick one up and hit them with it.

In this context it is not surprising that violence erupts between groups of young people. For example, Rebecca, and Charlotte, both aged 14, each described an incident involving their brothers:

> My brother got battered 'cos he had new trainers on as well
> – he had new trainers and all these lads came up – well there
> was a group of three of them, he was only sixteen and they
> were about twenty-odd, and all but battered him and then
> robbed his trainers.
> *(Rebecca)*

> I mean like on Christmas Eve my brother got his head
> kicked in just looking at someone walking past him – 'cos he
> was with this girl and they started on this girl and my brother
> said, 'That's a girl, that's not right', and that was it. They just
> got him.
> *(Charlotte)*

Personal safety in the area is certainly not guaranteed, and young people have to learn to look out for themselves in certain vulnerable situations. This is true for both sexes, but young women in particular tend to see public spaces as generally dangerous. The girls in the research by Burman and others (2003) could identify certain public spaces where they saw greater likelihood of encountering physical violence such as certain streets, parks, stations, and moving from one area to another. For Kimberley in the Respect study, looking out for herself meant not riding on the top deck of a bus:

> If you're by yourself you shouldn't sit on the top of the bus
> because people come on and go upstairs and just batter you
> and the driver doesn't even do anything about it.
> *(Kimberley, aged 13)*

It is a common occurrence that with the provision of few facilities for young people, they will inevitably congregate together on the streets or in the parks and there will be some sort of trouble, as Charlotte and Kimberley, 13–14-year-olds from this area, complained:

> **Charlotte:** 'Cos like there's nothing to do and then we're
> like always getting in a load of shit.
> **Kimberley:** But the police are always closing (the youth club)
> down so we've got nowhere to go.

Even going to the park can be hazardous, although with few facilities there may not be much else to do. Charlotte again:

> I mean I've not been to the park for ages but there's a lot of fights that go on in there because people hear that you're having fun – that's it 'We're going to come and wreck your fun now'.

In this North of England location there was a local gang culture, and fighting was commonplace (as also illustrated in the chapter on fighting). As in Northern Ireland, the desire and perceived need for revenge or retaliation for these kinds of violent activities was high. Things could escalate and get out of hand, as Jack and Mat (12–13-year-olds) endorsed:

> **Jack:** So you batter someone like they'll get people to batter you, then you'll get people to batter them.
> **Mat:** Just go on until –
> **Jack:** – and it's just going to go on – keep on going till someone gets killed or something.

In another group, the young men supported revenge as justifiable, especially if this was in the context of 'defending yourself':

> **Bobby:** If someone like batters your brother or sister, you've always got to protect yourselves, so you go back and batter them.
> **Interviewer:** So violence for revenge, is that good or bad?
> **Andy:** It's all right.
> **Greg:** It's all right as long as you're defending yourself.
> *(14–15-year-olds)*

As many in the Respect study asserted, violence can be morally justified if it is for self-defence (or the defence of another person). For Greg and his friends, this may well include revenge. The young people in this area similarly expressed little confidence in the police to take any useful action.

Down in the south of the country, on the streets of London, although not living in what could be described as a culture of violence, Harry was aware that there were groups and gangs in his area who had a violent reputation:

> …like when we're in school everyone's all happy in one nice
> community, but on the streets it's like big gangs and people
> come to stab you up.
> *(Harry, aged 12)*

When asked whether there was a difference in the way violence was seen inside
and outside school, 12-year-old Laurence commented:

> …if you were in school, yeah – and, right, say in school
> you've got like, there's like two hundred people – you've got
> about three people with a penknife. You go outside and
> you've two hundred people and like enough of them have
> got penknives, machetes in their pockets. But in school
> they've just like got one or two people…
> *(Laurence)*

It is significant that in the OCRCL survey, violence and safety in the streets of
London were the biggest concerns of the children and young people taking
part. Many were afraid to be out, and one in ten had experienced or witnessed
violent incidents (Sharpe 2002a).

In the areas described here, whether violence is driven by politics, sectarianism,
or poverty or a combination of these factors, young people have to negotiate
their personal safety through the streets and the public places like clubs,
football grounds, and even in schools. Other researchers have described
evidence of how young people traverse such contested spaces (for example,
Watt and Stenson 1998). With today's technology, mobile phones have not only
become an essential tool of communication between young people, but have a
role in their safety (Henderson, Taylor and Thomson 2002), although
conversely, young people may also be mugged for their mobile phones. The
situation in Northern Ireland has been and to some extent still is one of
extreme violence which has included petrol bombings, shootings, beatings and
so on. The level of violence in the North of England site was relatively lower.
There was a great contrast in the Respect study between these locations and
others, especially the Home Counties, where the young people lived in fairly
well-off families, in an attractive environment. The area may not necessarily
have a wealth of facilities, but the young people themselves have a much higher
quality of life, and one that is not characterised by violence. While all children
and young people should have the right to be 'safe' where they live, this right is
often bypassed on the streets of areas like those described in this chapter. They

have to learn where to go, or more relevantly, where not to go, and this represents a serious circumscription of their freedom. Young people enjoy a variety of increased freedoms today but freely walking around the streets, for many, is no longer one of them.

Key points

1. Sectarian violence in Northern Ireland is fuelled and thereby legitimated to some extent by many things according to the young people, including a continued historical and political momentum, bitterness, the media, football rivalry, and sectarian jokes.

2. Young men are more constrained in this culture of violence than young women because those with any community reputation or standing become guardians of the territory. Young women are freer to move around, cross boundaries or leave altogether.

3. Although some suggest more integrated areas and schools, they are well aware that mixing community relationships is dangerous because they can provoke violent reactions from family, friends, and even strangers.

4. Acts of violence against one group legitimate acts of revenge in return and validate a cycle of tit-for-tat activity that is hard to stop and fuels bitterness and aggression.

5. Many of these young people did not wish to bring up their own children with this level of violence and the legacy of bitterness and hatred, in the way that they and/or their parents had been brought up. They hoped to do things differently.

6. In Northern England it is poverty and deprivation, and lack of facilities in the mainly working-class areas that contribute most to produce violence in the streets, experienced by many young people.

7. In both locations, a mistrust of the police and a belief in their relative ineffectiveness in helping in violent or other situations legitimates taking action into their own hands (violent as necessary).

6 Violence in the media

> I think generally people are mature enough to realise that
> fighting's a bad thing in real life but when you're playing
> computer games it doesn't really matter because it's all just
> a game.
> *(Sam, aged 12)*

There has been a long-standing debate and research into to whether watching violence on the media has a harmful effect on children and influences their behaviour and moral values. The results have been inconsistent (Buckingham 1993) and many investigations imply no significant effects because most children learn to distinguish between fantasy and reality, and also suggest that the consequences may be more dependent on what an individual brings to what they are watching. For example, a violent film may possibly make a violent person worse, but not have significant effects on those with no particular violent characteristics. In exploring children's attitudes to media representations of sex, race, violence, and social class, Tobin (2000) suggests that children are not passive recipients of media values but form their own interpretations of what they see. In this context, some people looked to blame the killing of James Bulger on the young killers' viewing of adult horror videos, as Elliott, aged 13, from the Respect study, observed and rejected:

> **Interviewer:** There's a lot of fears aren't there, like being
> violent around movies, with kids watching movies on videos.
> **Elliott:** Like James Bulger? Yeah I think that, but they can't
> really blame it on you, you know, they blamed it on 'Child's
> Play 3'. Like his dad had about 300 horror movies in his
> cabinet. It might have been his dad who was a bad person
> and I don't know, showed opinions to the kid.

This chapter looks briefly at the areas relating to this issue discussed by the Respect young people that essentially focused on computer video games. These appear to be more popular with boys than girls, although one researcher (McNamee 1998) has suggested that although she found girls said they liked playing computer games as much as boys, that their brothers were controlling and policing their access to computer and video games in the expression of their masculine identity. In the Respect questionnaire, 73 per cent of the young men compared to 39 per cent of the young women said they 'sometimes' or 'regularly' played computer games. They were also asked to give their favourite of several types of media, such as films, TV programmes, and computer games. Violence did not in fact figure greatly in these. Their favourite films spread over quite a large number of categories, but action/adventure was the most popular (14 per cent), followed by comedy. Films characterised by horror and/or violence only accounted for 5 per cent of their choices. Of their favourite computer games, the most popular choice was for the quest type of computer games (21 per cent), and 10 per cent chose those centred around fighting. Some of the frequently chosen computer games were titled 'Street Fighter'; 'Mortal Combat'; 'Killer instinct'; and 'Command and Conquer'.

In their general discussions of issues that related to the relationship between the popular media and morality, the Respect young people tended to deny any suggestion that this would encourage violence in themselves, or otherwise affect their views on violence. While often acknowledging this as a possibility, they exempted themselves from this, perhaps because it implied a lack of agency and independence (Thomson and Holland 2002). But they were happy to discuss it as something to which children younger than themselves might be susceptible. They adopted an adult position as more mature beings relating how younger siblings or other young children might act out sequences or fantasies from films, cartoons or computer games, while they knew better. Tobin (2000) also found that the children he asked about imitative violence said that they were immune, but that other, generally younger children were vulnerable. They, like Zach, assumed that the course of moral development with age would mean that children would learn right from wrong, and reality from fantasy:

> It would only really encourage little people 'cos when they
> get older they learn right and wrong and things, not to
> shoot people like, those sort of things.
> *(Zach, aged 13)*

It was in several of the focus groups that young people discussed the statement that 'computer games encourage violence'. They asserted that violence in computer games was frequently viewed as just that – a game. The young people morally defended certain computer games that were defined as in their province, while implying the negative moral influence of examples of other computer games, as well as TV, newspapers, etc., that were perhaps placed more within the wider 'adult' popular media context. Elliott, who was 13, considered that 'at our age' there was no problem with violence and computer games:

> **Interviewer:** Do you think you are learning about violence playing these games?
>
> **Elliott:** No, no way. Most of the games you're blowing up like killer mutants. OK, say if there was a game like you're raping a woman or something, OK then, yeah, I suppose, I dunno. I don't think computers – I suppose like if you don't understand it, like you were much younger, but at our age I don't think there's much point putting on like a 18 certificate on a game.

What age they mean by 'younger' seems dependent on the age of the person talking, as 15- to 16-year-olds talked about 13-year-olds and younger ages as being vulnerable, while the 13-year-olds referred to those younger than them. Most seemed to think that 'younger' children may not tell the difference between fantasy and reality, and that their parents should monitor what they see. It also seemed that boys were more attracted to and tolerant of the violent nature of some media than girls, a not surprising finding, also commented on by Terry, aged 15:

> **Interviewer:** So what type of person, do you think lets it [violence in computer games] influence them? Do you think there is a type of person?
>
> **Terry:** I think it's younger children, mainly boys. Because like some of the Year 8s and Year 7s they play computer games and they like act out parts of it like, they all like fighting games – they do act out parts of it but…

Computer games relied on a 'self-immunity' founded on an ability to distinguish between reality and fantasy. This ability was a requisite for restraining the highly realistic graphics of certain computer games in the realm of fantasy:

> **Gareth:** If say a nine-year-old is playing a computer game where you shoot and kill, then they might think, of this looks fun – I'll go out and try this and they might be encouraged to use guns.
>
> **Miles:** That's not necessarily very true because it's just entertainment only, they just like sit there and play and have a good time, go away and do something else.
>
> **Andrew:** It depends how realistic it is, because if it's really realistic they may think, go out and do it, but if it's really unrealistic, they think, oh, shouldn't do that, I won't do that because it's too unrealistic.
>
> *(14–15-year-olds)*

It has been suggested that violence in the media may have some negative effects, for instance, if a person already has a propensity for violence, or if they are a certain type of personality. In relation to this, 16-year-old Owen told of how his friend's younger brother was playing one of their father's certificate 18 games called 'Grand theft auto' when his father was out. He described its content: 'It's got swearing and everything – (the guy) runs round punching people, they swear back at him, he gets in cars, run people over and you pick up machine guns and you shoot people, you shoot the coppers, get inside the cop car and everything'. Owen implied that the violent behaviour he saw in this young man (punching people in the street) may be associated with his isolated existence playing these computer games:

> And I've actually see him start walking down the street punching people and swearing so – his dad's gonna have a talk to him – he's kind of a lonely person, he just sits in the house and plays on his computer – he ain't got many mates, he's my mate's little brother – and he's only about that big.
>
> *(Owen)*

How young people acquire some level of 'immunity' to any kind of media influence was not really forthcoming. In the context of computer games, discussion tended to shift to the question of regulation and certification and the need to ensure that younger children were denied access to games for older ages:

> Well, I think that if younger children get hold of older
> children's games then – say a nine-year-old got hold of a
> fifteen-year-old game – then he may be encouraged to sort
> of play that game in real life.
> *(Gareth, aged 14)*

Jeremy brought in the role of family background in determining relative powers of moral distinction:

> It depends like what their background is if they think that's
> – if it's all right to go round shooting people or whatever
> you're thinking about...Well if like their mum and dad think
> that's all right and stuff like that, y'know just...they just, they
> don't really care.
> *(Jeremy, aged 12)*

Some young people considered other possible responses to the media. Owen suggested that children who act out games do so because they identify strongly with a certain character as they are envious of that character's power:

> I think it's more to do with envy...they're envious of the
> person, the power that they've got.
> *(Owen aged 16)*

Other young people diversified the discussion into other sorts of media violence, such as that in the movies. Colm considered that there was a lot of violence in the films he watched. Asked if he thought this was right, he replied:

> Nah, it isn't because there's people getting killed and all and
> children are watching it too. But there's some films – there's
> some films that isn't a true story but when you're a wain, you
> don't know whether they're true or not. It's only when you
> get to this age, when you get to about 13 your mammy tells
> you that them films are not true, all that there. You get to
> know...If your mammy said to you it's not true like, you still–
> you wouldn't believe her. You'd still have dreams about it.
> *(Colm, aged 13)*

Steven discussed this issue in a group of 14–15-year-olds in the North of England school:

> I think [violent films] are wrong to a certain extent…if you can handle the violence in it, well then it's OK, but then you see people copying off films – and I think they shouldn't watch them if they can't handle the violence. [Handling the violence means] well, you know, you just don't go out and copy it – you just watch it and…erm, be offended to some point but…don't take it to heart, because it's only a film – and some people have done that, done killings, which I think is wrong…it don't [have an effect] on me, I don't – erm, like these horrors and violence you see you know they're not real and just silly really, what they do.
> *(Steven)*

Perhaps being able to 'handle the violence' means that you have become toughened up to it, maybe linked in a way to the notion that being bullied can somehow strengthen a person. Conversely, if you 'can't take it' this implies some weakness or immaturity.

In 13-year-old Elliott's view, the immunity process started taking place through seeing violence in film, so that 'real' violence, such as shown on news or documentaries, ceased to have much of an impact for being real rather than fantasy:

> **Interviewer:** Do you think it's going to disturb a child or young person if they're seeing those sorts of horror films?
> **Elliott:** Yeah, it makes them become, what's the word, less conscious of violence, so when you see it on the news and it's really happening you don't care that much, you put a blind eye to it…

He reflected on his transition to a more mature position, from when he was younger and more sensitive to items shown on the media:

> I have changed now, I watch like 18 movies and play games like 'Resident Evil 2' and that like I used to, when I saw a little panda on a wildlife programme getting eaten by a lion I would have nightmares and nightmares for like a month and I was much more sensitive, but now, I don't know if it's

because I've grown up or not, I don't know what to blame it
on, but it does make you much less sensitive really.
(Elliott)

For a few, like these 12–13-year-olds, TV coverage of sport was viewed as having
at least an equal potential influence for violent behaviour as films or computer
games:

> **Shirleen:** I think there's influence in sports as well because
> that's what children do – like say they're watching football or
> something and they could hit the referee and then they'll
> think it's funny. And in boxing as well – boxing is the worst.
> **Trevor:** That's what happened in this football match. Guess
> what, the referee, yea? – the man kicked the ball in his face
> and he got knocked out.

The young people here did not discuss the whole range of media, but it is clear
that they did not consider themselves vulnerable to media influences and this
includes the proliferation of computer games that many, especially the boys, are
involved in playing. Once again, gender plays a part. Certain aspects and areas
of media consumption are gendered, and thus violence tends to be coded as
male, whether it is represented in films, computer games, videos or sport.
Similarly, we have seen in other chapters how young men are more involved
than young women in fighting and community violence, and how male bullying
is generally more physical than female bullying. In young people's eyes, media
violence may not have an influence on their own behaviour, but the consistent
representation that identifies violence with masculinity continues to endorse
violence as appropriate male behaviour in the 'real' world.

Key points

1. The Respect young people were aware that violence on film, TV, or video
   games might affect the attitudes and behaviour of the young. However, they
   never considered that they were the 'young people' who these were going to
   affect. It was always others, younger, and in their view, more vulnerable and
   less mature than themselves, who were the susceptible ones.
2. In terms of sensitivity to effects, it was suggested that programmes showing
   cruelty or violence in nature and wildlife could have more impact on the
   sensitivity of some young people; or the violence inflicted in sport by players
   or fans, than the violence contained in fantasy films and video games.

7 Conclusion

From these chapters we can draw out some overlapping moral threads that run through the young people's narratives, and see what kinds of situations legitimate the use of different levels or expressions of violence. It appeared that they had already absorbed views about moral development and in the domestic context most had adopted a more traditional moral position expressed in the need for parents to use a certain level of discipline. They endorsed parental discipline (but not too much) so that children could learn right from wrong and to stop them from doing 'bad' things. This was seen as involving low level violence such as a slap, and was in contrast to research describing the views against this expressed by much younger children (Willow and Hyder 1999). Parents had the moral authority to slap them but other adults did not.

A related finding to emerge from the Respect study was that the moral values of these young people were little different from those of adults (McGrellis and others 2000). The popular assumption that the general moral values of younger generations are in decline was not endorsed from their judgements of what is right or wrong. Moreover, it was interesting that when some of them interviewed an adult (mostly their mother) about changes in various areas of social life including violence, both generations tended to agree with the idea that young people had too much freedom and too little discipline and this had contributed to apparent increases in crime and violence.

The young people saw no moral grounds for bullying – it had almost no legitimacy, although they conceded that a bully could attract a following, and some young people (both the bullies and the bullied) rationalised the possibility of a kind of character strengthening effect for the victim. It was seen as morally right that people should 'stand up to' the bully, or defend the bullied, or tell on the bully, although the latter was easier said than done as it could result in the whistle-blower becoming a subsequent target. There was some overlap in the behaviour and moral codes relating to bullying and fighting. Using violence in self-defence was a very acceptable reason or excuse, as this clearly involves 'standing up for yourself'. Community violence added to and widened the moral boundaries. In a situation of community hostilities, defending yourself or members of your family and the family honour was almost an imperative. Although there were mixed feelings about the use of violence in revenge, this was often seen as a cycle that was very hard to stop.

These young people described many intricate dilemmas and contradictions in their relationship with violence outside the home and in the community that make it more understandable, although no easier to deal with. 'Standing up for yourself', and thereby gaining the respect of others in situations of violence was very important in a variety of situations, although some acknowledged that this was often hard to do. Respect was a quality seen to characterise both sides of violence. For example, a good fighter got respect for this skill and especially if it were used to defend weaker others against bullies, but sometimes a kind of respect was afforded to the bully for his/her power to hurt physically or verbally. This gave rise to a confusion of fear and respect. There was no shortage of stories of violence, and prospective actions in response to it. Such 'fighting talk' had some currency and there was a form of culture around this. Although there is not necessarily a direct link between talk and reality, it could serve functions of, for example, self-expression, or moral communication.

Media violence was mainly discussed with respect to computer and video games. More young men than young women played with these and this was linked to their expression of masculinity and level of control over this medium within their households. In terms of moral values, the young people of every age saw themselves as being 'mature' and therefore unlikely to be influenced by such media violence, and identified younger people as the ones who would be vulnerable.

Gender and location were important factors, and in judging issues of violence, the young women were more disapproving than young men. Yet many young women were no strangers to some level of violence in terms of fighting, especially in locations where there was a high level of violence. Two of the locations in the Respect project were characterised by cultures of violence – Northern Ireland, and a disadvantaged working-class estate in the North of England. The attitudes and experiences of the young people growing up in these environments, and the meaning and validity of violence for them were different from those young people in relatively non-violent locations. Social class and location interact, as also shown in other issues such as sexual practice (Thomson 2000b). Social class also played a part here and the better-off, mainly middle-class young people from the Home Counties location were less acquainted with, and suggested less physical ways of dealing with violence.

One of the strongest themes to emerge in the Respect study was the ubiquity of violence in many of these young people's lives. It could be encountered anywhere such as in the home, from peers, the police, gangs and crime in the community, and through political violence in Northern Ireland. Although young people generally disapprove of violence, and recognise its ultimate ineffectiveness, in everyday life they inevitably encounter incidences where physical or verbal violence cannot be denied or avoided, and some are rationalised or defended as justifiable. These experiences are significant in their understanding of moral development and values. They are negotiating contradictions and competing values. The social, situational and spatial background to any incidence of physical or non-physical violence is important and any incident may be more complicated and involve more moral issues and different perceptions of moral authority and legitimacy than is apparent from the outside. It is hoped that this 'thinkpiece' has helped to illuminate the understanding of violence in various contexts through the eyes of these young people and will usefully inform policy and practice around these issues.

References

Borg, M (1998) 'The emotional reactions of schools bullies and their victims', *Educational Psychology*, 18, 4, 433–44

Buckingham, D (1993) *Children talking television*. Falmer Press

Burman, M, Brown, J and Batchelor, S (2003) '"Taking it to heart": girls and the meaning of violence' *in* Stanko, B *ed. The meanings of violence*. Routledge

Calouste Gulbenkian Foundation (1995) *Children and Violence*, Report of the Commission on Children and Violence convened by the Gulbenkian Foundation

Campbell, A (1989) *Girl delinquents (revised edition)*. Blackwell

Cohen, P (1997) *Rethinking the youth question: Education, labour and cultural studies*. Macmillan

Connolly, P, Smith, A and Kelly, B (2002) *Too young to notice: The cultural and political awareness of 3–6-year-olds in Northern Ireland*. Belfast: Community Relations Council

Cutler, D and Frost, R (2001) *Taking the initiative: Promoting young people's involvement in public decision making in the UK*. Carnegie Young People's Initiative

DfEE (1999) Social Exclusion Unit, Home Office and DoH, Circular No. 10/99, *Social exclusion: Pupil support*. DfEE

Elliott, M (2002) *Bullying: A practical guide to coping for schools*, 3rd edn. Pearson Education

Epstein, D (1996) 'Keeping them in their place: hetero/sexist harassment, gender and the enforcement of heterosexuality' *in* Adkins, L and Holland, J *eds Sexualising the social*. Macmillan

Epstein, D (1997) 'Boyz own stories: masculinities and sexualities in school', *Gender and Education*, 9, 105–16

Epstein, D, O'Flynn, S and Telford, D (2003) *Silenced Sexualities in schools and universities*. Trentham Books

Flood-Page, C and Taylor, J (eds) (2003) *Crime in England and Wales 2001–2002: Supplementary Volume, National Statistics, January 2003*. (http://www.homeoffice.gov.uk/rds/pdfs2/hosb103.pdf)

Frosh, S, Phoenix, A and Pattman, R (2002) *Young masculinities: Understanding boys in contemporary society*. Palgrave

GALOP (1997) Homophobic youth violence survey, cited in ESRC Violence Research programme, *Taking stock – what do we know about interpersonal violence?* ESRC, June 2002, p.18

Gill, M and Hearnshaw, S (1997) *Personal safety and violence in schools*, commissioned by the Suzy Lamplugh Trust, Research report No. 21

Glover, D and others (2000) 'Bullying in 25 secondary schools: incidence, impact and intervention', *Educational Research*, 42, 2, (Summer), 141–56

Hari, J (2002) 'Ulster lives out their Groundhog Day', *New Statesman*, 25 February, 32–3

Harrington, V and Mayhew, P (2001) 'Mobile Phone Theft', Home Office Research Study 235

Henderson, S, Taylor, R and Thomson, R (2002) 'In touch: young people, communication and technologies', *Information, Communication and Society*, 5, 3, 494–12

Holland, J, Thomson, R, Henderson, S, McGrellis, S and Sharpe, S (2000) 'Catching on, wising up, and learning from your mistakes: young people's accounts of moral development, *International Journal of Children's Rights*, 8, 271–94

Home Office (2001) *Criminal Statistics England and Wales* cited in The ESRC Violence Research Programme *Taking Stock – what do we know about interpersonal violence?*, ESRC, June 2002, p.14

Katz, A and Buchanan, A (1999) *Leading lads*. Topman

Katz, A, Buchanan, A and Bream, V (2001) *Bullying in Britain: Testimonies from teenagers*. Young Voice

Kelly, B (2002) 'Young people and sectarianism in Northern Ireland', *Children Now*, 13, (Summer)

Laberge, S and Albert, M (1999) 'Conception of masculinity and gender transgressions in sport among adolescent boys: hegemony, contestation and social class dynamics, *Men and Masculinities*, 1, 253–67

Lamplugh, S and Pagan, B (1996) *Personal safety in schools*. Arena

Mac An Ghail, M (1994) *The making of men: Masculinities, sexualities and schooling*. Open University Press

McGee, C (1997) 'Children's experiences of domestic violence' *Child and Family Social Work*, 2, 1, 13–23

McGee, C (2000) 'Children's and mothers' experience of support and protection following domestic violence' *in* Hamner, J and Itzin, C *Home truths about domestic violence*. Routledge

McGrellis, S (2002) 'Pure and bitter spaces: identity and territory in Northern Irish youth transitions', Young people 2002 Conference, Keele University, 22–24 July

McGrellis, S (2003) *Managing sectarianism and violence: Young people in Northern Ireland – a study over time*, in the London South Bank University series of Working Papers

McGrellis, S, Henderson, S, Holland, J, Sharpe, S and Thomson, R (2000) *Through the moral maze: a quantitative study of young people's values*. The Tufnell Press

McNamee, S (1998) 'Youth, gender and video games: power and control in the home' *in* Skelton, T and Valentine, G eds *Cool places: Geographies of youth culture*. Routledge

Mellor, A (1999) 'Scotland' *in* Smith, P K, Morita, Y, Jungar-Tas, J, Olweus, R, Catalano, R and Slee, P eds *The nature of school bullying: A cross cultural perspective*. Routledge

MORI (2000) *Mori Poll for Youth Justice Board*, 27 March

NCH, Is it true that children can be bullied online and via mobiles? http://www.nch.org.uk/itok/showquestion.asp?faq=9&fldAuto=145

NISRA (Northern Ireland Statistics and Research Agency), www.nisra.gov.uk

Office for National Statistics (2000) *Living in Britain: results from the 1998 general household survey*, cited in Crompton, L (2003) *'It's Got to be Real ... Really Real'* – *Report on Consultations with Young People about Alcohol, Alcohol Education and School Policy*, Drug Education Forum

Oliver, C and Candappa, M (2003) *Tackling bullying: Listening to the views of children and young people*. DfES and Childline, March

Rigby, K (2002) *New perspectives on bullying*. Jessica Kingsley

Samaritans, *Youth and self harm: Perspectives. A summary of research commissioned by Samaritans and carried out by the Centre for Suicide Research, University of Oxford* (http://www.samaritans.org/know/pdf/Selfharm%20report%20summary.pdf)

Sharpe, S (2001) *More than just a piece of paper? Young people's views of marriage and relationships*. National Children's Bureau

Sharpe, S (2002a) *Sort it out revisited*. Office of Children's Rights Commissioner for London

Sharpe, S (2002b) *'"It's just really hard to come to terms with": young people's views on homosexuality'*, *Sex Education* (special issue), 2, 3, 263–77

Sharpe, S and Thomson, R (forthcoming 2004) *All you need is love: The morality of sexual relationships through the eyes of young people*. National Children's Bureau

Smith, P K (2000) *Bullying in schools*, Highlight No. 174, National Children's Bureau

Smith, P K, Morita, Y, Jungar-Tas, J, Olweus, R, Catalano, R and Slee, P eds (1999) *The nature of school bullying: A cross cultural perspective*. Routledge

Swain, J (1998) *'What does bullying really mean?'*, *Educational Research*, 40, 3, 358–64

The Mirror, 16 September 2002, pp.1, 4, 5 and 6

Thomson, R (2000a) *'Authority' in Rutherford, J ed The art of life: On living, love and death*. Lawrence and Wishart

Thomson, R (2000b) *'Dream on: the logic of sexual practice'*, *Journal of Youth Studies*, 4, 4

Thomson, R and Holland, J (2002) 'Young people, social change and the negotiation of moral authority', *Children and Society*, 16, 1–13

Thomson, R, Holland, J, McGrellis, S, Sharpe, S and Henderson, S (2001) 'From Peter Andre's six-pack to "I do knees": the body in young people's moral discourse' *in* Mulburn-Backett, K and McKie, L *eds Powerful bodies: gender, sexualities and embodiment.* Macmillan

Thomson, R, Holland, J, Henderson, S, McGrellis, S and Sharpe, S (2003) 'Researching childhood: time, memory and method' *in* Allan, G and Jones, G *eds Social relations and the life course.* Palgrave/Macmillan

Tobin, J (2000) *Good guys don't wear hats: Children's talk about the media.* New York: Teachers College Press

Watt, P and Stenson, K (1998) '"It's a bit dodgy round here": safety, danger, ethnicity and young people's use of public space' *in* Skelton, T and Valentine, G *eds Cool places: Geographies of youth culture.* Routledge

Willis, P (1977) *Learning to labour.* Saxon House

Willow, C and Hyder, T (1999) 'The myth of the loving smack', *Childright*, 154, (March), 18–20

Women's Aid Federation of England, *Domestic Violence Statistical Factsheet – Children August 1999* (http://www.womensaid.org.uk/dv/dvfactsh3.htm)